Lost Lake

Folk Opera

Spring-Summer 2018   Volume 5 Number 1

In This Fifth Anniversary Issue

Six Poets Laureate

Short fiction & essays

Poetry

Everybody has one — Op-Ed

SHIPWRECKT BOOKS PUBLISHING COMPANY L.L.C.
Rocket Science Press
Lost Lake Folk Art

Up On Big Rock Poetry Series
Lost Lake Folk Opera

Lost Lake Folk Opera is a Shipwreckt Books imprint
published twice annually.
Letters to the editor are always welcome.

309 W. Stevens Ave.	Rushford, Minnesota, 55971
507 458 8190	contact@shipwrecktbooks.com
Managing Editor	Tom Driscoll
Publisher	Beth Stanford

www.shipwrecktbooks.com

WWW.SHIPWRECKTBOOKS.COM

Cover art & interior graphics by Shipwreckt Books

MIDWEST
INDEPENDENT
PUBLISHING
ASSOCIATION

Council of Literary
Magazines & Presses

[clmp]

INDEPENDENT BOOK
ibpa
PUBLISHERS ASSOCIATION

US Press
Association
Registered
Member 2016

INDIE
BOUND.org

US Press
Association

PEN
AMERICA

The Freedom
to Write

PEN
PROFESSIONAL
EDITORS NETWORK

www.shipwrecktbooks.com

The Bear Husband
Ken McCullough
Winona, Minnesota, Poet Laureate

John Osa and the Village Girl

Prologue

She lived in a town by the western sea,
silvered by wind and salt air.
The men set out in their boats each day
and the women mended the nets.

The last few months the catch had been lean
and the skies were black as soot.
The waves had swept fishermen overboard
and the wails of the women rose.

*

One day in late summer she wandered off
to pick blueberries in the woods.
They were scarce, 'til a dark young man
said I'll take you to a patch.

So they climbed the hill to a meadow,
and they picked through the afternoon.
They lost track of time, and didn't say much.
The berries were dusty and big.

The air was dry so she took off her dress
and filled it full of berries.
She didn't mind that he saw her naked--
he was naked too.

And then it started to rain in sheets--
He said you won't make it home--
the river's swollen its banks … I'll give you
shelter, a fire, some food.

He smelled strong, like upturned earth;
he smelled like the dance of danger.
But she was a dancer and followed him home.
She spent the night, a month, another.

Drawing by Julia Crozier

*

She danced with his brothers at gatherings
some black, some brown, some yellow,
some red, and even a few albinos.
The gamut, from lean to stout.

Some came in gaggles, some alone,
they came from all directions.
Some had little ones at their dugs,
and they quaffed from drinking gourds.

They danced and they danced and they swirled her around
clumsy but somehow agile.
Some even stood upright on hind legs
just to make her feel welcome.

Then they'd drop to all fours, swing heads back and forth,
and bare their teeth at each other.

Sang on the intake of their breaths--
huffed and chuffed in low voices.

*

He had a den that he shared with her,
he'd marked it off with his urine.
The den was a quiet place for them
in the shadows to lie together.

The smell of him, of her, the earth,
the music of wind in the pines
and the cheerful black-capped chickadees,
elk bugling over the hills.

When they coupled he made love to her fiercely:
he took her from behind,
biting, growling, with claws dug in;
there was thunder all around her.

She'd had a husband for just three months
who'd drowned in his fishing dory.
But this kind of mating was new to her--
this butting, this caterwauling.

She turned him so they looked at each other
and she gazed him tender and slow.
A rumble came from deep in his chest--
they were thunder and starlight together.

Unlike a male and female bear
they wanted to stay together.
And that bone in his penis, new to her,
was her single-minded consort.

She noticed the footprints of her bear--
just like a barefoot man.
Her own were somewhere in between
that of a bear and a woman.

She slept with her head on his chest
rough against her cheek.

She heard the drumbeat of his heart
that pulled her down to sleep.

*

She taught him how to light a fire,
he taught her to catch fish with her hands.
He came to like roasted trout
and she learned to like raw liver.

Often he took her to honey trees,
but she let *him* collect the honey. Oh, Honeypaws!
Once he fell with a thud to the earth
with a beehive stuck on his snout.

They roamed together most of the time
but sometimes he went alone,
passing through groves like a hairy ghost,
a shadow, and barely a whiff.

The same hawk always circled them
and the black jay made his reports.
As they rambled, she always left traces.
He noticed, but looked to the side.

On cold clear nights with the stars awash,
the coyotes called and answered.
The scent of black cherries on the wind—
she learned to scent them also.

When the air turned chill, they ate their fill,
and fattened up for each other,
but they went to separate dens for the winter.
He was John Osa, she was Ursula.

*

A light snow had fallen. John Osa
walked backwards out of his den.
Then jumped to his left to a smaller cave
in case they'd been following him.

Spring

Ursula (sung softly):

Woodpecker rapping on a hollow tree
Drip drip dripping outside
the belly of sleep is open wide
The long red dreaming is over

Two balls of fur with needle teeth
are sucking at my breasts
One of them has his barrel chest
The other looks just like me

I'll sup buttercups, buds of willows
cool water from the pine bog
rake up ants from a rotten log
moss under paws for pillows.

Human voices in the distance:

A hunter(shouts): The dogs have picked up the scent.
Another hunter(shouts): Look up there, on that ridge!. . .

Ursula (spoken):

Do I hear dogs? And hunters' voices?
Surely they're looking for me.
And they're looking for meat, but he
will fight them. There'll be no choice.

John Osa appears on the sheltering ridge.
(He speaks, obviously disturbed):

I thought our bond would protect us.
I wondered if they'd find you.
It is not bear nature to stay this close
but I wanted to see my two sons.

Some male bears even eat their own spawn
but that isn't my inclination;
I am here to protect you three--
you are not yet fully a she bear.

(he sings):

They waited for the snows to clear.
How did they know to look up here?
Do you recognize their voices?
We're running out of choices.

Ursula (spoken):

I know they are my brothers.
My cousins are some of the others.
They're looking for both of us.
What we have is turning to dust.

John Osa (spoken, angrily)

I don't know whether to trust you!

Maybe you'll give me away!
Maybe this is our last day!
Maybe these poor cubs
will fall victim to their clubs.

Ursula (sung):

My Honeypaws, my dearest
I tell you this in earnest
Their voices are fading, they're going away
They will not find us today.

But the fish are gone, they are starving,
the crops in their fields have withered.
I must tell them to follow the polestar.
I must lead them to where you are.

John Osa (spoken, in a rage)

How can you do this?!
(He growls and rakes the ground with his claws.)

Ursula (sung):

I am caught between two worlds—
Do I have a choice?

John Osa (sung):

I see the way it must be--
The grandfathers have set me free
to honor these prayers. Must I give
my life that their families may live?

I thought that there would be time.

Ursula(sung);
 My soul tells me otherwise.

 You will be the epitome
 of everything strong and good.
 These cubs will grow into bearhood
 and honor the ways of this world.

John Osa and Ursula (sung, together):
 Part of us will be together
 Part of us will go on forever
 Though we're human and bear
 The stars won't care;

 These sons will carry us skyward.

Epilogue

Ursula:
 He put up a fight and I was there.
 Watching from back in the trees.
 He looked in my direction. That question
 in his eyes as he died.

 Almost as if someone had written it,
 he'd taken down three of the dogs.
 One of my brothers lost an eye,
 a cousin, two of his fingers.

 They skinned my bear, and his naked body
 looked like a giant man.
 They cut off his head, and pulled out his claws
 cut the bone from his penis.

 They called him their Elder Brother
 and asked him for forgiveness.
 They took turns touching his head
 and they all began to sing.

 They didn't dress him there in the woods—
 they carried him back to camp.
 They cut him up and roasted him—
 It turned me inside out.

His hide, they stretched out between the trees,
but his bones they kept from the dogs.
There was laughter, singing and drumming
and someone played a flute.

The hunters each wore a pair of his claws
and moved as my bear had moved.
The hunter who'd struck the killing blow
wore the penis bone on a cord.

Three other hunters danced like dogs
to honor the dogs that had fallen.
I stole away from their celebration
Under the waning moon.

I burned his head, his beautiful face,
with that look of resignation.
I blacked myself with his ashes,
and wailed to the beat of their drums.

I took his skull from the ashes, painted it
red, with black eye rings.
I placed it high in the crotch of a tree
facing the mouth of our den.

*

Gulls skreeled in the air and followed me
up to my family's house.
My mother was there, and my little sister
and we hugged for the longest time.

My mother asked me many things
about my time away
but I was afraid to tell her much
for fear of what she'd do.

People were always staring at me
and laughing behind their hands
the kids pretended to be bears
and pestered me mercilessly.

The men talked low and made their bets—
which one of them would approach me.
But I stared at them until they gave up;
Not one of them had enough courage.

As days went by, I fought with my family--
my temper at a boil.
I felt so alone—I just wanted to hide
and leave my shame behind me.

One day I took a swipe at my mother--
then EVERYONE was afraid.
The dogs tucked tail and ran away
then my brothers drove me out.

"Our sister's become a bear."

*

His spirit came to see his sons
who both are strong and curious.
One has his eyes, the other, mine,
but both have his raven-black coat.

My milk had the taste of hickory nuts--
somewhere between bear and human.
But he never had a chance to taste it
before they hunted him down.

I had taught them not to trust their cousins
down in the human village.

They whined like dogs when I turned them out—
it hurt my heart to hear them.

They hunted together for several seasons
until one of them took a mate.
He tried to introduce her to me
but I just turned away.

When maples turn red I think of John Osa
as the sun slips to the west.
I can sometimes feel his breath on my face
When he presses up against me.

*

If you decide to marry a bear,
never return to the humans.
Settle in and raise your cubs,
under the Bear in the Sky.

This piece is based on a story that is common to the oral traditions of a number of North American native traditions, even down into Mexico, as well as in other places, like Siberia, Scandinavia, and Europe in general, where bears figure prominently in their mythology. The most complete version of the story, from a Yukon Tagish source, is recorded in David Rockwell's *Giving Voice to Bear*, Roberts Rinehart, 1991

Six Poems
Steve McCown

On Visiting an Ex-Drama Student in Jail

The yellow brick road
you starred on
ends here:
in a six by eight-foot cell.
I won't lecture you;
you are beyond that now.
Nor will I say that jail time
is like class time as others have said.
In these endless hallways
I am a stranger myself,
ignorant and scared.
I only know that your monkeys
are descending, tearing apart
your vital stuffing, and flinging
it over unknown fields.
You have set yourself on fire,
and each piece of your sand
peers out of a clogged hour glass,
building up slowly inside
until the upper half threatens to break.
Let it flow freely again,
in your time, on your watch,
beyond this dark castle.

The Glue Sniffers

We heard them first,
like bellows slowly worked,
fanning dying embers

or iron lungs
compressing and expelling
regulated air.

A music of sorts
they made, a doomed duet—
two microphones left on in the dark,

amplifying stifled background sounds.
Then we saw them:
their breathing brought life

to paper, the brown grocery bags
caving in over their mouths,
then wrinkling out slowly,

the sides and tops quivering like cauls.
Their covered heads were
hidden in contained clouds,
the fumes of glue swirling
with each breath
like waves collapsing on themselves.

They sat side by side
against our school,
their legs sticking out straight as planks.

A near perfect tableau:
nothing moved except paper,
nothing heard save bagged breath,
nothing seen except eyeless masks.

Eleven and twelve and thirteen,
we held our breaths
all the way home.

Where to Find Wildlife in Minnesota

Off Highway 61,
check out the trash barrels along the Mississippi River.
Raccoons will stare up at you.
Tip the bin over for a closer view.

Pull into a Duluth gas station
and park next to a black bear,
spread-eagled on the hood of a Jeep.
You can touch it while filling up.

Walk the old wagon wheel bridge
outside of Winona
and see eel and gar writhing on the defunct road.
Leave them there! Garbage fish.

At the bottom of dumpsters in Rochester,
elegant deer legs,
sawed off,
grow longer or shorter,
depending, every time you look.

For fascinating remnants—dark green,
intricately patterned, pottery-like—
exam my neighbor's driveway.
He loves to park the wheels of his sports car
on the massive shells of migrating turtles.

Scour the mowed ditches for pheasants,
shredded like Oriental fans,
or stare up at the heads
staring down at you in any bar.

Look in a mirror,
look at pictures of yourself as a teenager.
Don't bother with the North Woods.
You won't see them there.

Raft

In memory of Celia

Why did you do it?
Why did you jump raft?

You knew well its roughhewn craftsmanship,
everything tied together
with hurried knots that held fast, that persevered.
Humor and conscience, you said, propelled the timbers.

You knew well its humanity,
Huck and Jim on a floating stage,
creating dialogue,
crossing boundaries together toward unmapped regions of becoming.

I saw those characters emerge vividly
from your writing's cross-ties.
I heard them clearly
in your essay's buoyant words.

Why did you abandon Huck and Jim,
who were your true kin?
You dove into darkness
and swam toward the coldest shore.

Math Lesson

Outside of Red Wing,
on a motorcycle,
I veered off blacktop
onto loose gravel.

Like Orpheus, I had looked back,
to see if she was still there,
when I felt rocks instead of road and arms.

At 65 mph, at 18 years each,
we flew to 55,
the large black numbers on the speed sign,

upright like an immense flashcard
constructed out of steel.

I couldn't brake on gravel;
feet from a simple math lesson,
I somehow eased us back onto Highway 61,
relieved to feel concrete and hands again,
to see numbers only and always in retrospect,
and to move with the loving, slowly,
as he had hoped before turning his head.

Full Circle

Running over the dead
or the still breathing,
immobilized mid road,
we stay with those animals
for miles even as we drive ahead.

They stick with us, too.
Once, after hitting an elk square,
Already dead, with all tires
(no time to brake, swerve, pray)
I pulled into a final rest stop

on the edge of a dark city.
The tires, rims, lug nuts,
and chariot-style spokes
were still bleeding,
and those were the visible parts only.

That night, in a red darkness,
I dreamt of wheeling full circle
again and again.

Forever travelling breathless up

Anne Muccino

From the novel Red Bricks, a Rocket Science Press new fiction release scheduled for Fall 2018

Dalia

I was born in the brumal season in the time of the otter when the ground breathed snow and ice and earth's awakening was not yet contemplated by the dormant clay, and what saved me in that difficult breaching was the power of my water totem. So my *abuelita* says. For it is she who examined the placenta then washed the umbilical cord and buried it in the fields, not in the corner of the house where the feet of women

Photo by Dan Coffey

are rooted. Like Moses who struck the rock twice, she doubted the strength of my place in this world and sought to lift it where rain reaches and my totem can breathe. It is from this, my mother says, my rebellion comes. It is why in my younger years she found me in the night standing outside the house in the nakedness of a storm, drinking its music. And like Moses, my grandmother was punished for her sins by not living long enough to see the fruits of her labor ripen. There is no going back and undoing what is stone, and I thank her every day.

I have lived in Las Cruces, New Mexico for as long as I can remember, and longer even before that. My dreams take me to these same streets, this same place, but in these dreams I am dressed in pants with a vaquero's hat that sits worn on my head and my name is Lucas. I am not so tall, but taller than most, and the dream ends the same each time in the streets of Las Cruces where I am shot dead with a bullet to the heart and then I have no further memories of that life. But I do not expect to, because I am dead.

H ere my name is Dalia. My mother is a Nahua half-blood and married my white father two years before I arrived. My eyes are the dusky green of tortoise shell and my hair is the color of iron rusted in salt water and when the boys come they ask to touch it to see if the fire is hot on their hands. We live on my father's ranch in a stucco house painted white with a red tiled roof now the shade of salmon where the word "Paraíso" is lettered in the wood that shadows the entrance. Here I am not encouraged to wear pants and my father says I must marry. My 15th birthday approaches in the spring, and at that time I will be prepared in the ways of women so that I will not embarrass my family or my future husband. My father says that he did not make these rules, that these rules existed even before he was born and that he does not have the power to change them. I see in my mother's eyes that she does not agree, that she once stood where I am now and longed for the freedoms I desire, yet she will not oppose my father. And when I say 'nantli, you must help me,' she turns away and stares through the window to the south where her people come from, and I know that her mind is set. In this way I am alone.

It is a hard thing, to hate one's own father, the man who taught me to ride, the man who loves my mother, the one whose seed I spilled from. The laws of nature forbid it and I feel I am forever travelling breathless up the backwards slope of a mountain with only small hope to hold. Moments I think it impossible to hate him; moments I know it is impossible not to. This is why I must believe in God. Because I pray every day for a miracle to change my father's heart. And because He has bent down to kiss the earth with the spirits of its beasts; knowing that I will live forever if I can always feel the girth of a horse between my legs. That is the Lucas in me.

J.T.

They carried them from the well to lay at the foot of his grave, hoping thieves wouldn't steal them in the night. Dusty red adobe bricks. Baked in the heat of the New Mexico sun, the deep color of a roan quarter horse, brushed 'til its sides shined.

Granddad would have liked that, the simplicity of a man's mark in the world boiled down to a heap of red bricks. It said something about him. About his tenacity, his slow nurturing patience that allowed him to go forward while others stalled. Something a carved piece of granite couldn't say. He never tired of getting his hands wet in the muck of earth and water, and their rooted solidness bore him on when the outside world wore him down. He was humbled by the land and the way it sang to him when his hands heaved the clay from the sweltering ground, shaping his future, brick by brick, waiting for them to dry in the oppressive desert heat.

J.T. loved that old man.

They stood at the rim of the hole they dug, but not too close. Yesterday's rain made the ground soggy and weak under their feet. The unearthed dirt stank of pitch and darkness and of things that never see light. Nine feet of hole severs you so completely from a loved one that you almost ache to crawl into the hole with them. *Almost.* At the same time truth motions you to step forward in line because you're that much closer to the grave yourself. Joke's on you. Granddad would have laughed at that. Would have said there was no getting around it. If you worry about it, you die. If you don't worry about it, you die. What's the point? It's what you did in the time before the dying that mattered.

Harlan's roughed hands curled the brim of his hat. J.T. knew he wanted to say something more than the obligatory prayers. Something important that would last and cause them to pause when they thought back on this day. But Pa hollered at them to "hurry it up" and "we ain't got all day," and Harlan can't think well when he's under that kind of pressure. When Pa turned to go, Harlan cleared the tightness in his throat and spoke. "You stay dead, ol' man." And that made Pa laugh, a little *heh heh* sound they weren't expecting. Both boys fixed him with a hard look to see if he had been drinking.

Funny wasn't in the way Harlan meant it—J.T. knew that. His brother loved Granddad as much as he did, maybe more. It was just Harlan's way of telling him to rest easy, that there was no sin in wanting to escape this life. They understood the misery of sitting in a wheelchair day after day, bearing witness to the ruin and neglect overrunning the homestead he sunk his heart into, watching all he worked for collapse. Watching Pa abandon the land and indulge himself, spending money on god knows what. Harland and J.T. knew what, but they weren't to say it out loud. No man should have to tolerate suffering like that just because they've outlived the use of their legs. That last year Granddad was already living dead.

"And whatcha bring those bricks out from the well for? They don't belong here." And before they could stop him, Pa picked one up and dropped it in the grave. A dry thud echoed as brick thumped the pine coffin and lay still. J.T. looked to Harlan and saw the muscles in his jaw working and the thin line that was now his mouth. Then Pa looked up at the sky and told them to move along, those were rain clouds setting in and wouldn't that just be the shits if they got caught in the middle of a bucket down with a half-dug grave. "I'll be waiting in the truck," he said.

J.T. hated that old man.

Harlan put his hat back on and glared at Pa's back, then picked up two spades and threw one to his brother. They began to shovel the unearthed dirt back into the hole. The hollow sound of earth making contact with the boxed coffin undid J.T. some, and he was glad when they finally reached the point where dirt was hitting dirt. This was his second grave digging. The first was Ma's when J.T. was ten, a sound he hated even more back then.

When they got back to the house, Pa told them to listen up so they took seats at the table while he reached for the whiskey bottle. He brought down three glasses from the shelf.

"You boys gonna hear about this sooner or later, so I might as well tell you now." He poured the whisky into one of the glasses and drank it down. Then he refilled the glass and the others next to it. "I'm selling the ranch."

They stared through him like he was a ghost. He lifted the whiskey to his lips a second time and threw it back.

"You can't do that," Harlan said.

"Shut up," Pa said. He slapped the glass down on the table, making the drink in the other two jump. Then he leaned across the table towards Harlan. "Last time I needed to check with you, boy, about what I can and cannot do was *never.*"

A sudden stillness entered the room and J.T. felt the electricity between them spark like a live wire

being tapped. It didn't take much to set Pa on edge, especially after a day of drinking, and they knew the danger in offering up any kind of resistance. He'd seen Pa bully Harlan before. But this was different. There was a growing up to Harlan J.T. hadn't noticed, and he could tell his brother wasn't backing down. He could see it in the way Harlan's elbows dug deep into the table, and the naked heat he directed at Pa. It wasn't long before he heard the scrape of Harlan's chair as it pushed back and he made to stand. "It ain't your land to sell," Harlan said. "He wanted it to stay with us."

No one spoke. Then suddenly Pa laughed, only this time it was a raucous laugh that shook his throat. He put the whiskey bottle to his lips and took a swig, wiping his mouth with the back of his hand, the smile disappearing from his face. From his jeans he pulled a pocketknife and picked up an apple from the basket on the floor.

"You'll always be the fool, son," he said, narrowing his eyes at Harlan. "I don't know what that ol' man told you, don't care. This ranch is mine and there ain't a damn thing you can do about it." The knife cut a slit deep into the apple's skin. He broke off a chunk and stuffed it in his mouth, licking the juice off the blade, all the while keeping his eyes on Harlan. "Set yourself down."

There was something familiar about the temperature rising in a room that came from growing up with it, and when he was young J.T. couldn't ignore the swell of adrenaline dribbling into his veins that interrupted the living of an ordinary life. It promised the spark of something new. But that changed the night Pa's drinking got out of control and Ma got hurt, and they all came to realize how dangerous living in a pressure cooker can be, and the truth of how they were all sitting atop a bundle of dynamite with Pa holding the matches. A cold fear that moved with them throughout the house, throughout their lives, making the tiniest change in routine a threat. It changed the way J.T. saw the world, and from that day forward he got to trembling inside each time he felt it enter the house.

The day she got hurt was the day Granddad came back to life. He came out of his wheelchair and stood between them, shaking with such fury that the finger he pointed at Pa was wobbling and little bubbles of spit formed in the corners of his mouth. "If you ever … "he said, his finger folding back into his hand to make a fist. You could see the veins in his forehead throb. "If you ever," he repeated, "touch her again…," then his words trailed off and stopped, like he wasn't sure what came next. His eyes swept the room and took in Ma on the floor bleeding and Harlan at ten years old kneeling beside her, and J.T. eight years young in his PJ's trembling.

"I'll *kill* you." He said these last words in a low voice that had lost its roar but none of its promise. Pa didn't speak. They stared at each other while time stood still. The world was silent with the sounds of Ma crying. Then Pa walked away.

Only this time it wasn't Granddad, it was Harlan, and J.T. knew with absolute certainty that Pa wasn't walking away. Inside he felt the buildup of the tremble threatening to climb out of him all day. He rose to his feet on shaky legs, not certain which way the dynamite was going to pitch, and what side he was supposed to be on. And just when he thought all hell would break loose, the world lit up outside like it was daybreak and a roaring boom ripped the sky. In the next instant the pounding of thunder hammered the roof of the house like a stampede of horses. The storm had broken free.

"Shit," Pa said. "Those calves are loose in the south pasture. Gotta get to `em before they drown."

He was right, there was no room for arguing. Those calves had to be found. But J.T. could see in Harlan's face that it was hard to surrender courage when it's just gaining breath—you just never know when you're going to find it again. A weariness came over his brother as Harlan reached for his hat, and J.T. knew the fight had gone out of the room. At least for now.

"J.T., run out and turn those horses loose," Pa said. "If lighting hits the barn, they can't be hemmed in."

Harlan shook his head. "No way a truck will make it down the embankment in this rain without sinking in the muck," Harlan told Pa. "Going to have to saddle up, old man. Best you take care of the horses in the barn and J.T. and I will collect the calves."

Pa's back straightened and his eyes went cold. "I was born on a horse, boy," he said, "if there's any saddling up to be done, I'll be part of it."

Harlan looked hard at Pa, then past him to his brother. He saw the begging in J.T.'s eyes, pleading with him to step down. In that moment he understood what 17 years of this living had cost his brother. Had cost them both.

"I can handle the horses," J.T. said.

"I know you can," Harlan said.

"Then whatcha waitin' for?" Pa said.

Harlan ignored Pa and looked straight at J.T. "You come along after you loose the horses, but stay clear of the creek. It'll be swollen. Don't take any chances, you hear?"

"I hear."

"If one of those calves go in, you let it go, understand?"

J.T. nodded.

"Don't be stupid."

"I won't."

"Stop yapping and get to it then," Pa said.

Those were the last words J.T. ever heard him speak.

A wide arc of lightning passed overhead as J.T. made his way to the barn, and it wasn't but two seconds before he heard the clap of thunder ride up behind it. He heard the whinnying of the horses and their hooves tap-tapping the ground as the thunder cracked. He opened the barn doors wide and stepped in, the dark musk of the horse muddied stalls pushing against him, the rain in the air making it sweeter. It brought him back to Granddad and how the man craved leaning into that smell every chance he got. He said it gave consequence to his life and reminded him every day that horses were a gift from heaven. Pa said the stink of livestock always brought him back to the slaughterhouses his family sent him to work in when he was a boy spending ten hours a day shin-deep in blood.

J.T. opened the first three stalls and the horses bolted, kicking dust as they broke. They didn't need his permission. In the next two stalls he had to do some persuading. He coaxed the black bay and the mare out with help from the thunder that rained down hard again, so ear-splitting he saw white. When he swung open the last stall, J.T. could tell Ruby was staying put. She had backed into a corner of the stall and was shivering from head to toe.

"Come on, baby," he whispered trying to sweet talk her into moving, but her eyes were wide like they'd been stretched flat against a sharp blade. Her breathing was grunted and heavy, and he knew she was in a bad place. He'd have to ride her out. J.T. grabbed her halter off the hook and came close, holding out his hand so she could smell it, all the while her snorting and stamping with those wide eyes. Just as he slipped it over her head she jerked away, but still he managed to grab hold of her mane. As he swung himself up onto the sweatiness of her back, a spool of thunder rolled over the roof again and he felt himself lift into the air as she reared and flew forward like a coyote on fire. They crashed out of the stall and he thought for sure he was going to lose his grip. But the rhythm of her gait was like breathing to him, and instead of fighting he gave into it. They soared out into the husk of the storm, the unexpected relief of rain pelting their heads and draining their thirst. The air was thick with water, and there was no seeing through it.

The darkness of the downpour made J.T. lose his bearings and he was helpless to steer her in any one direction. He called out to her above the rain, above the thunder and the lightning but if she heard him, she refused to listen. Both of them soaked to the bone and still she kept going. He pulled up hard on the halter, shifting his weight over her haunches, bearing down to signal her to stop, but she refused. Lightning charged and he could make out the outline of the old sycamore tree. That's when he knew they were headed towards the creek. J.T. knew the creek would be swollen. He couldn't let her take him down into the muddy water where they'd both surely drown.

"Whoa," he yelled about a dozen times but she kept on. And just when he'd made the decision to surrender, to let go and take his chances hitting the ground, a bolt of lightning lit up the night and she came to a dead halt. For a moment J.T. thought she had been struck, the way her hooves fastened to the ground and her body went rigid. He was re-centering his weight when another zigzag of electricity ignited the sky, and that's when he saw them.

Pa stood in the distance, his arm across his forehead trying to ward off the blow. Next to him must have been Harlan, his raised arm coming down towards Pa with something solid; something

that squared in his hand. A rock, no, ...a *brick*. Then the lightening blew out and there was only darkness and rain until he and Ruby took in the thunder and he felt himself tumbling from the horse as it reared. He didn't remember meeting the ground. A loud buzzing in his ears cancelled out everything. Everything except the splash of water and Ruby's whinny as she disappeared into the creek. Then the world disappeared.

J. T. woke up two days later and knew Pa was dead. He knew this because sometime during those forty-eight hours Pa had passed through his dreams—sat on the rim of them begging J.T. to make the journey over to where he was sitting. Holding out a piece of black licorice in his hand. J.T. could see the black clouds gathering behind him, and something in the way they knew his father scared him. It was the kind of dream that makes you wake up reaching for the light and feeling drained out of yourself, relieved you were on solid ground. Only he couldn't wake up; not then. And when he finally did open his eyes, every fiber in his body was alive with the knowledge that he came just *that* close to never waking up again.

He didn't see Harlan in his dreams, so it hit him hard when they told him he was gone.

"What do you mean, *gone?*"

They stared him down, studying his face, trying to read something that wasn't there, trying to decide if they were reading it right.

"He's dead J.T."

At that moment the floor at the pit of his stomach gave way and he felt hollow, less than a whole person. Like he was holding something in his hand and it just vanished. *Poof.* He could almost hear the word inside his head, helping him to understand that part of him just broke; a small hiccup in the heart's rhythm that stifled his breathing, just for a second, when he tried to stop time and realized he couldn't.

Everything the sheriff's men said after that felt tired and far away. How they found Pa sprawled out on the granite ledge overlooking the river, a few yards from the sycamore tree, his skull caved in. They assumed he lost his footing and fell, hitting his head on the rock. How they found Harlan on the south side of the creek in the shallow reeds lining the riverbed, Ruby's halter tangled in his arms. It looked like he drowned trying to save her, but they didn't know for sure. They tracked where his horse's hooves went in from the north of the river. That didn't sound right, given what J.T. saw, but he didn't say.

He told them what he remembered. How the storm got out from under them, and how Pa and Harlan went to rescue the calves, how he freed the horses and fell from Ruby, and how everything went black after that. He left out the part about the raised brick, figuring whatever he thought he saw in the lightning of a rain-cussed sky was no more reliable than his dream vision of Pa beckoning him towards hell.

"What?" they asked.

"Nothing."

"You got somethin' more to say, say it."

"I got nothin'."

"You sure?"

And just when he thought they were never going to let up, the tall one in the back with the sideburns told them to lay off; he had just lost his whole goddamn family for chrissake.

By the time the ranch sold, the snow had set down on the ground in small pockets of white gauze, so delicate looking you wanted to scoop them up with a butterfly net. The sale took longer than expected because of the conditions he laid down. The graves were not to be disturbed. J.T. had bricked a low wall around the perimeter and it now looked a proper cemetery. Whether the new owners would honor those conditions he had no idea, but he set it down in writing, and in his head it was done. He buried Pa out in the south acre underneath the old sycamore tree. A lot of folks thought that was disrespectful, not including him with the family, but those who knew Pa weren't surprised. It was J.T.'s business

and he got to thinking he'd sleep easier if he knew the rest of them weren't spending eternity lying next to the devil.

The money from the sale of the ranch paid off his father's debts and left J.T. with a small pocket full of cash. He wasn't sorry he sold it. He didn't want to be living with the ghosts of his past the rest of his life. He knew Granddad would want him to live his own dreams and not get wrapped up in holding a place for his. He planned to head west towards California where he heard the land was fertile and its beauty something to behold. He couldn't allow himself to think about Harlan yet and let the finality of his being gone sink in. It might open a floodgate he couldn't dam back up, and it scared him. Afraid it would drag him under and if that happened there was nothing and nobody that could get him up again. Truth was, he recognized death calling when he heard it and knew he had to move along or get swallowed up in grief. Laying down ain't in the Swain boys. Harlan taught him that.

J.T. walked Ruby out of the stall and stopped to tighten the cinch. He swung up into the saddle and nickered her forward, looking towards the west, feeling the weight of uncertainty on his shoulders. Yes, Ruby survived the storm. If it was Harlan's doing, he'd never know. It seemed a whole lot of foolishness to risk your life over a horse and Harlan would have known that. J.T. kept wondering if during those two days there was a small part of him that passed through Harlan's world while he was getting back to his own, but he couldn't bring it forward in his mind. He hoped it'll come back to him, like a slow memory that blows out of the dust, and you have to stop to remember whether it really happened or you dreamt it, or both. His mind hadn't summoned it yet, but he had time. And that was a good thing.

Forty Lenten Haiku

Lee Henschel Jr.

Author of *The Sailing Master, Books One & Two,*
(Rocket Science Press 2014 & 2018)

1.
in the blue jungle
where ancient spirits dwell
there rings a tiny bell

dawn spreads across the Negev
to reveal the coming day

2.
Sea of Galilee,
placid, blue, God's own daughter
blood in the water

3.
in the hushed air,
in the sleeping shadows,
in the dry scent of cedar

4.
you feed the latent fire,
and within the small flame
everything has found its name

Nazarenes gather at the well
coming to fetch their water

5.
some call you messiah, some say heretic,
son of god, son of man
both begotten and made

6.
but Mary knows you well
long before you knew yourself,
so restive in her womb

7.
your first breath
the first hungry cry
of an artless child

8.
no one to interpret
no one to guide
left on your own

9.
left to your imagination
left to wander on your own
with no instructions, only a vow

10.
a forthright child
humble, and of low birth
no king on high

11.
Nazareth and Capernaum
your humble beginning
your love of the poor

12.
your first stumble
not on Calvary's steep slope,
but as you learn to walk

13.
when you were a child,
and watched the storm clouds racing
did you know, even then, how it would be?

14.
but for now
you only play in the sun
Mary's precious child

15.
Joseph, teaching you his trade
the feel of heart wood
the balance of a well made tool

16.
but you're a dreamer
never focused or attentive
always elsewhere

17.
dreaming of some kindness
unexpected and unforced
done for the sake of doing

18.
stark moon, sentient shadows,
the slow waltz of candle light
a form of prayer

19.
in the deepest shadow
awaits the transubstantiation
as Mary mourns her son

20.
your flesh
consumed by those who would love you
and your blood, drunk by the same

21.
the moment will surely come
when Peter turns his back
and Pilate stands aside

sacrament of awareness
devotion to the moment

22.
warm rain upon your skin
the touch of a wordless prayer

23.
in the Sinai
lost in the searing heat
your fears rise

24.
the Essenes bring you here
to deny you food and water
and to purge you of your fear

25.
not the fear of dying
but the granularity of your death
filling the cup

26.
a woman stands alone
a desert rose in her hand
she does not know how it will end, only where

count the sabra
count the dunes

27.
the agony
the fear rising at Gethsemane
will death will be everlasting?

when you thirst,
will the Roman bring only gall?

28.
your heart, pierced through by a spear
the centurion comes to break you legs,
to make sure you are dead

29.
Father,
deliver them from fear
bless them with your grace

30.
I thank you for my life, for my life
I will be hear now
be hear now

31.
to honor it
to nurture it
to share it

32.
for the sake of their well being
so they will meet along the way
and help each other, help each other

33.
if not with compassion,
then with kindness
if not with kindness, then gratitude

34.
so unlike the Pharisees
who say no
when all along it is yes

35.
satellites cross the night sky
weeping, unveiling the spell

36.
to reveal our blue marble
placed just so
in heaven's open field

37.
a dominant gene
an earthen jewel
never to be seen

38.
when you arrive in hell
what will Lucifer say?
that the children will be first to die

39.
in the blue jungle
where ancient spirits dwell
there rings a tiny bell

Columbine, Red Lake, Sandy Hook,
Marjory Stoneman Douglas

40.
arise, but not just yet,
serve the poor, for it is late
the stones in this stream do not wait

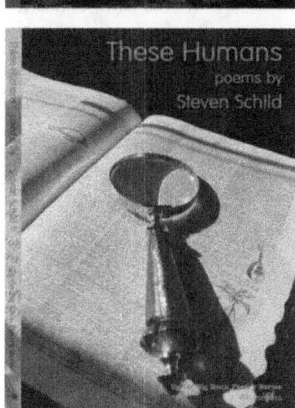

Relapse
Christopher G. Bremicker

I'd gotten over a huge hump in life and thought I had recovered from my nervous breakdown. I'd been sick forty years. To celebrate, I decided to have a drink—after twenty-five years of sobriety.

I made this decision at night, when I got over the hump. I knew to never make big decisions at night. Wait until the clarity of morning, my brother, who was an administrator by profession, advised. I knew this but got out of bed, put on my clothes, and headed for a bar.

First, I called my Alcoholics Anonymous sponsor to notify him of what I was doing. I got his voice mail, left a message, and thought he was in bed. He turned off his cell phone at night, I thought.

The first order of business was to get some money. I did not have any cash on me and did not know if bars took credit cards. So, I walked to the Super America gas station a block from my apartment building and took out sixty dollars from the ATM. I did not know what a drink cost these days, it was so long since I drank.

I took the bus toward downtown. I was excited and scared. I felt like I was going to basic training in the Army. I decided on Louie's Bar, but the bus stopped at Smithy's for another passenger and I got off. It looked like a friendly place and Louie's was a Hell hole. I opened the door of Smithy's and walked in.

I outgrew bars at the time I quit drinking. If I did not outgrow them, I would never have quit. I used to love the places, from cement floors to chrome and glass.

I expected Smithy's to be crowded with people having fun. There were a few people in the corner, next to a pull tab booth, and the bartender was picking up salt and pepper shakers. He wore an argyle sweater tucked into old blue jeans.

I took off my coat, placed it on the back of the bar seat, and sat down. I felt at home. The bar was dark and neon signs lit it.

I ordered a Manhattan. I told the bartender I wanted cheap bourbon, with bitters, cherry juice, and a cherry. "What kind of vermouth do you want?" he asked.

"Sweet," I said. He looked under the bar and found a bottle of sweet vermouth. "What kind of bourbon are you using?" I asked.

"Makers Mark or Jim Beam," he said, to give me a choice.

"Which is cheaper?"

"Jim Beam."

"Use Jim Beam, please." He made the drink.

My twenty-five-year Alcoholics Anonymous medallion hung on a chain around my neck. I considered taking it off and placing it on the bar. I considered telling him about it.

He placed the drink in front of me and I laid a twenty-dollar bill on the bar. He gave me change. The drink cost seven dollars. When I drank heavily, they cost one and half bucks.

I sipped the drink. The alcohol burned my tongue, scalded my throat, and warmed me. It was a cold, wet April night. I could taste the bourbon, sweet vermouth, and cherry juice. The drink was delicious. I was not used to the burning sensation and liked it.

There was a baseball game on the television over the bar. The Giants were playing somebody. I loved to watch baseball and watched the athleticism of the players as they batted, threw a man out at first, made a double play, and pitched. The players were young, in wonderful physical condition, and their skill was hard to believe.

I sipped the drink. The bartender moved around behind the bar and people behind me talked softly. It was a quiet weekday night.

I began to feel the effects of the booze. I was getting happy, emotionally full, and my imagination began to soar. I nursed the drink.

Then I slid it out from me and in front of the bartender. "Do you want another one?" he asked.

"Yes, please," I said.

"Same way?"

"Same way."

He made the drink, put it in front of me, and withdrew a ten-dollar bill from the money I had on the bar. He placed the change on the bar with a flourish. "Thank you," I said. I did not forget how to drink at a bar and was making a Chinese tea ceremony out of it.

The second drink got me drunk. I continued to watch the game. I began commenting on it. "Don't swing on that pitch," I said, or "They got him!" as they threw a man out at first.

Then I lost track of the game. Someone hit a double and drove a man in. One man caught a flyball in right field. I did not know what the score was.

I sipped the drink, noticing only the burning alcohol, the taste of the Jim Beam, and the sweetness of the drink. It was a good Manhattan. Manhattans were strong drinks.

My A.A. sponsor called. "What's going on?" he asked.

"I'm having a drink at Smithy's," I said. "You're welcome to come down."

"Are you all right?"

"All is well," I said. He hung up. I set my limit at two, before I left my apartment, and that's where I stopped.

I left the remainder of the money on the bar for the bartender, used the restroom, and weaved past the bar and out the door. I weaved down the sidewalk and stood at a bus stop. I was drunk, babbled to myself, and weaved around the bench of the bus stop. There was another Super America near the bus stop and its lights went out as I waited for the bus.

The bus arrived, and I staggered onto it. I did not remember the ride home but had the wherewithal to pull the cord at the right stop. I weaved home, took the elevator to the tenth floor, entered my apartment, and took my laptop downstairs to our community room.

I began to work on an art history paper. I was taking a class at the university and was rewriting a paper on which I got a poor grade.

My sponsor called again.

"Where are you?"

"I'm at home, working on my art history."

"Good," he said. "I'm glad you're home."

"That textbook you bought me ruined my life."

"What do you mean?"

"I have to study now. Without it, I would have blown off the course."

"I'm glad you're okay. Call me in two days."

I was too drunk to think. I went to bed. I was nauseous as I took off my clothes. I got into bed and fell asleep. In the morning, I had no remorse.

I thought about myself for a while at my daily devotions. I had no consequences from the night before, except a slight hangover. I had a headache. I did not lose my family, driver's license, or job.

I had another kind of responsibility. I had friends who depended on my sobriety. I resolved not to tell them. Nor would I tell my brother, whose reaction was unpredictable. He was an A.A. Nazi and devoted to its principals. I made a mental list of who to tell.

I met a woman once at an A.A. convention who relapsed after thirty years of sobriety. She showed up at a restaurant, where she was a waitress, drunk. She laughed about it. The impact of my behavior did not sink in yet.

I contemplated my spirituality. A.A. was a spiritual program because alcoholism was a disease of the soul. That's why they called booze, spirits. I did not feel guilty, at least yet. With human contact, my guilt might surface.

I wore my sobriety on my sleeve like a gold cufflink. Now it was gone. I had less than a day of sobriety.

I needed to go to an A.A. meeting and confess. I needed a psychologist. Instead, I wrote this and went to class. Life went on.

At Starbuck's on campus, a young barista, who was excited about her job and life, looked at me with dismay. My inner peace and serenity were gone. I was tormented, hungover, and bewildered. I lacked the joy I exported once. To her, I was another drunk buying a cup of coffee.

I waited for the consequences to hit. At one A.A. club, I watched as its members pilloried a man who relapsed. I hoped it did not happen to me.

My belly, where my feelings of joy resided, was dead. My face, once filled with beatitude, was barren. I fell off the wagon.

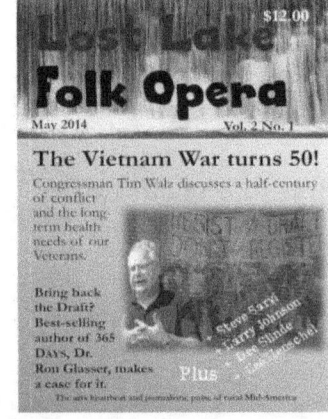

Three Poems
Tufik Y. Shayeb

Collision

watch for the stop sign etched in the
crease of my smile or else you might clip
the sharpest edge
of how I remember you most

crash into this conversation and
forget how the parts fit together
you may never feel whole again

I will bury your kinder words under a
snowbank beside the road hoping
they will keep, until summer
when things go back to normal

but when the dogs come scratching and
the piles turn into puddles
there is only barbed grass and gravel

the less-than-kind words those, I
will bury under the music of a song
that was suddenly paused
and picked up again on other side of years

for ten years a needle scratched the cd, dancing
never came easy in these shoes
but now I've learned to sway with memory

and with the other words the
middle words, the lean words the
words that catch the blows,
that fill the empty spaces of packages

the words that reconstructionists can't
figure out how to piece together, I don't

know what do with those words

so watch for the signs they are easy to
miss if you look away and, if you do,
you may never feel whole again

Green as Grinch

when I was seven the young,
Coiled Nerves Jacob
sprang, popped and pushed me

when I wasn't looking

and I suicide swan dived from the
orange peeled monkey bars
of Elementary School

into the pound-flat mat,
covered in sand and twigs

I broke a few things that day,
a back, a rib and a funny bone

now, every time I hear a joke, I'm
not really sure what to do

so I hold my breath until my face turns blue,
and my eyes roll back under their lids

people say it looks like a corpse,
there're probably right

I'm rotting inside I'm vegetables gone bad,
no—no, I won't eat it inside

*

that Christmas my grandparents gave me
a green dimetridon named *Fred*

it would eventually become
the most important dinosaur of my childhood

one day, while at school, I was busy
taking assessment tests and Fred was
kidnapped from his cubby I assessed the
situation and sobbed, like thick lips
pressed
up to the thunk-thunk vacuum of sky

like space, French-kissing bronchials
leaving not a liter of air

to fill the empty, sucking nothing inside

she said it was my *own fault*,
because I brought a toy to school

but *he* wasn't a toy and *I* didn't bring him, he
was a dinosaur, he was Fred
and he was gone

        *

it would be another eight years
before the dreams began

the ones where I would say to her words
like *screw you*,
goddamn it, burn in hell, I hate you

now I use those words a lot people
say it looks unstable
and they're probably right

now, I'm a loose strap on a
straitjacket, and fairly certain
I lost a button last week

        *

I once asked my little sister to stop
complaining about her chapped lips,
but she didn't

so I switched her lip balm
with a glue stick

                    *

when I was seven, I stood in the
backyard one afternoon

and watched a determined boy
in corduroys

slam my pet rabbit on concrete
until its body became a red balloon

ruptured, breathless, and flat

it was late winter, he was nine
he wanted to show me his newest trick

                    *

by age twelve I insisted my
skin was green

I insisted I was seasickness,
money, trees, limes, green crayons, envy,

I was a green dinosaur

I was the Grinch who stole Christmas
every year for the rest of my life

and always, thinking of Fred, I stole candy,
because it felt like the right thing to do What

We Left Behind

This is it— the pillow where
pop culture rests is bobbled
head
and takes its final rasping breaths

This so-called antique mall,
so brown and still, brittle and

This is where I wrap my
wounds in nostalgia so tight, I
am mummified,
my organs in custard porcelain jars

Lost, the patrons belong here
and the isles are a sickening berth

With hats to match the six-foot
scale pencil that I would love
to hear snap,
cutting the cavernous, petrified air

I am lost but seeking here with
wired this, vinyl that

She complains about the young
couple of kids having too much
fun, *too much*
the fetish of old age distressed

Soft electric fans rattle and huff
wheezing from too much cigarette

The tired Jack, his neck turned like
some sleeping swan or goose biting
the edge of his tin-lid Box,
clucking an awful tune no doubt

And why are there skin and antlers?
So few things slither or trot here.

Frames, cabinets, and chandeliers too
many chandeliers—here— cassettes,
neon signs, helmets, and too few books,
coveted and saved.

Three Prose Pieces
Justin Watkins

Excerpt from the collection *Marks of Permanence,* an Up On Big Rock new release scheduled for Fall 2018.

John Bass

Cloutier found Bass in his lower deck cabin unlacing his boots. Both men were bleached and wind-worn having returned from a day on the big water adjacent to the Gulf. Bass looked up but Cloutier said nothing; he seemed to be just waiting. Bass said that he had been thinking for a long time about a shot of tequila. He didn't do that sort of thing all that often but he said he'd been thinking about it most of the afternoon and he'd decided he was going to do it. Maybe several shots with some of the salt and lime wedges in the captain's bar upstairs. Cloutier approved of the idea but declined to take part himself. He turned in the doorway to leave but Bass stopped him: I wish the gar had raked my face, he said. I wish he'd raked my face when he thrashed his way out of the boat this morning. Cloutier studied his partner but did not speak. Maybe three or four lines across here Bass said and pointed to his right cheek. A mark of permanence. Bass looked up at Cloutier who nodded in understanding and then left for the boat deck.

Disappointment Lake

That year there were forest fires. Great billows of white smoke overhead in place of clouds; a constant eye-stinging haze over the water. Fire burned around Pagami Creek and a passing fisherman had said that it wouldn't be out any time soon. On the fourth night camped on Disappointment Lake they heard noises at the water's edge. Cloutier walked to the beached canoes, searching smoke low over the water with a small point of light. A hollow sound like the beating of an empty drum led the beam between two canoes and the shiny shellback of a great turtle breaking the water surface. The smoke and light playing together gave the shell a mystical appearance: some beast come from gray depths attended by motes in air and in aqua. It's gleaming yellow eyes close-set and its carapace an old cross-hatch, plated and grooved and scarred. A water beast born of lake-stone, run over and worn down by the decades passing. The turtle moved its head in slow calculation. A bass on a stringer ferried backward and forward in fear, striking the canoes in a roughly-timed rhythm. Counting down its demise thought Cloutier. He called the others to the spectacle and they all came down to shore.

That a creature so barnacled and obtuse of body could move with such burst fascinated the men. After three lunges the turtle held the bass in its great beak, flattening its head unnaturally. From this point of advantage, the turtle brought forward one claw at a time, situating it to maximize the tearing and ripping pressure. Beak and claw rendered the fish into strips of white flesh. All the while, flashlight beams played through smoke and water, reflecting in its eyes, a genuine mythological beast. The snapping turtle hoisted its bulk over the torn fish, its head broad like an anvil, its clawed feet fanned out. The men studied the reptile, senior to all of them in years. Later at the fire Cloutier thought of the quiet lakebed and the accumulated silt where all turtles sleep out the cold. He pondered the turtle's homing call and subsequent discernment that led it to the fish on a stringer near the camp. In the morning Cloutier walked to the canoes. The stringer hung empty in the water. No remnant of the fish remained. The bass had vanished with the turtle as if it were never there.

Muskellunge

The man took the seat just left of Bass. May I, he said, but it wasn't a question. Bass looked away and then at the man: he was dressed in a plain dark shirt with a rigid collar and buttons down the front, in the fashion of an officer. His face was well built save for a missing eye, and his expression was flat in a sort of matter-of-fact projection that seemed to fit the interior of the dim and quiet room. Bass thought it a good setting for meeting a one-eyed stranger. He actually thought that sentence, but all he said aloud was, Sure.

They made some small talk and a few minutes into the conversation the subject turned to fishing: You know the place just south where all the muskies are piled up?

I do know it, replied Bass.

So you know they put those monsters in the pool above and in a sort of justice the muskies refused to stay there; they slid over and through the dam to the tailwater When we were kids we used to run up and down that river. The muskies just stacked in that tailwater. No one really knew how many. A dozen or a hundred. Or more. In a few hours of fishing we would move two or three, hook one or two and maybe land one.

One day, the man said, pointing to his puckered eye socket, I was fishing alone, casting an old wooden lure. Three treble hooks. A big nasty painted stick, really. Meant for heaving and mechanically retrieving what was essentially a battleship of barbed points. I hooked the first fish I moved, and after just a few minutes a muskie of exactly fifty-one inches lay at my feet in the shallows. I was able to get about half of it in my net. We don't have specific nets for every occasion do we. As you know. So this particular net was undersized given the task at hand of holding that giant fish. I knelt low to the limestone and got my right hand on the muskie's tail. I was backing it out just as it came clear of the net and it bucked against my touch, and its head launched against my face, and one of those treble hooks, those big mean bastard hooks, one them pierced my right eye. Barb pushed through.

The man paused. Bass looked at him and then down at his own hands. You can imagine what happened next, the one-eyed man continued, with that barb holding. You can imagine but I'll tell you anyway. Before I understood that was happening—before I could physically react—the weight of the fish pulled my eye from its socket. I groped about and dropped all my weight to the ground following the fish that's got my eye. The eyeball was still attached to my optic nerve, so I could still see through thick glass the face and eye of that muskie. It thrashed wildly and I pressed against it, calling out. Stuttering. The fish would go still for a second and then build to writhing. My hands couldn't manage the living fish and the dangling eye stuck on a barbed hook. I had to resist the urge to pull away. Finally I just bear-hugged that fish and squeezed with everything I had. I raised a stone and began striking that old dragon-head. Each blow of the rock brought a ringing pain to all my senses, but I kept on, trying to pin the fish down with my face while I bludgeoned at it. I could hear and feel the head breaking. But it was coming apart far too slowly for me, twitching through its expiration. I remember my ragged eye actually seeing with some blinking clarity fish scales as the body finally stilled.

Of course I then had to remove a barbed hook from my own eye. Well, I couldn't do it. Too many variables and too much pain. I don't know if I thought the eye could be saved, or if I was just too afraid to tear it from my face. I didn't stop to reason my decision to walk home in alternating fits of silence and wailing, my eyeball bound to the mouth of the now-limp fish. My father assessed immediately that the eye was lost. He cut through what he called the cordage and worked that night to clean and cauterize. We left the bloodied fish out on the porch floor. Lure in its mouth and my own eye speared there hanging from the jaw of a muskie.

The man had leaned in close to Bass and said, I had you as a man who might relate.

Yeah, Bass replied. I'm that.

Four Poems of the Road
Joyce Sutphen
Minnesota Poet Laureate

The Puzzle

If only it didn't change every
few minutes; if only the wind wasn't
a factor,

then we could look for that constellation
of birds in a tree, then we would see
the road

leading up the mountain to where
a small village is nestled into
a valley,

and someone is waiting for someone
(we don't know their names—
a mystery!).

Even the sky might make sense
if only it would hold still for
a moment.

Fargo Fandangle

In Fargo, there are no leafy
sea dragons floating in their
seaweed homes,
no seagulls circling the black steeple
of the Pontoppidan Lutheran Church
on 4th Street.

When the clouds break,
a shaft of sunlight
drops
like a ladder from some California
in the sky where we could drive
through hills the color of
ripened soybeans

and arrive at the vineyard gate,
ready to sail away in long boats
bearing an unmistakable resemblance
to Viking ships, their sails
as dark as wine.

In a Rented Car

She drives, and I watch familiar fields go by,
my foot rocking the cool cradle of my sandal.

The car is white with a blue interior. How like
a cloud it is, carrying us over hills, racing its shadow.

The years between our then and now are thin as paper;
we flip them back and forth like pages in a book.

After a fifty miles, we begin to tell each other the parts
of our lives we like best, we make pronouncements.

We come to decisions about things we have agonized over;
doubting, we invoke the ghost of time slipping away.

A hundred miles up the road, when the small
town of our childhood comes into view, we slow down.

The church steeple pokes above the roofs,
the water-tower lifts its paunch on thin legs,

We imagine walking up Main Street as if
we had no idea how soon we would reach the end.

It Was Like This

Driving, we did not count the miles
as we glided over concrete and tar
listening to voices on the radio and
in our cell phones or to the sound
of rubber and steel on the road.

We never imagined we would
have to stop this way of moving,
that we would have to step back
onto the earth itself, that distances
we once erased would reappear.

We thought we could drive our
Chevy to the levy forever; we
thought there would always be
gas in the tank, tanks in the ground,
and oil like five easy pieces

to keep us primed—just like
the way we thought our hearts
would always keep the beat and
bring the blood out and back
again to make us last forever.

My First Hunt
Jim Miles

Even before my first deer hunt at the age of 12, I had a history of hunting. It started when I was 3 and asked my mother to make a bow and arrow for me so I could go out into the woods to hunt for bear. She did... and I did. However, I never got a bear in those early years. She didn't know where my interest in hunting and the outdoors came from. My father didn't hunt and had no interest in it what so ever.

Maybe it was a genetic memory passed down from my grandfather... or maybe it was a past life thing. Native American memories also seemed to be a part of me. I knew how to construct wickiups, a sapling frame hut covered with long grass bundles used by many Indian tribes as a temporary shelter while on the hunt. I learned to identify buffalo trails in the fields behind our house and through exploration, discovered the animal tracks and lairs of the game in my immediate area.

The woods and fields were home to me—like part of my back yard. In those days, I and most of the neighborhood kids walked out of the house in the morning and followed our own interests and went our own way without parental supervision We did it all on our own.

When I was five, I broke my leg jumping off a wall into a pile of snow on a dare. Unfortunately, I hit the snow shovel, but even that didn't keep me inside. One day I decided to make an Indian wikiup in the back woods, about a mile and a half from the house. It was slow going with the cast and all, so I skipped going home for lunch to work on my project. This was very out of character for me. I always showed up for meals. I liked to eat! When I missed lunch, my mother panicked and called the sheriff. The sheriff didn't find me because my wickiup was in a hidden spot, deep in the woods. Even a five-year-old knows you don't build these kinds of sacred structures right out in the open. It had to be hidden … or so I thought. But come supper time I hobbled home for a brow beating from my worried mother. I didn't understand her panic. I was just out on one of my adventures … that's what I was supposed to do … it was my calling.

Throughout my teenage years and early 20s I spent almost every free day outdoors either hunting, fishing, or hiking in all the wild places that I could reach on my limited budget. It became evident to me early on that hunting was far more than the kill. The kill ended the hunt. It was the hunt... the adventure in the woods, fields, and waters that sang to me.

I loved the different colors of the changing seasons. The spring greens, the darker summer green, the brilliant red, yellow and tan of the fall and the white, grey and black shades of winter. It was a symphony of color that kept changing day to day. I was out in it every day and had the ability to see the beauty and the magic of nature's wonderland.

My walk home from school passed Grandma Larson's old place. She knew me well because I was friends with her grandson Steve. Together Steve and I shot bows and arrows, BB guns, and on rare occasions Steve's 4-10. We shot a lot of tin cans, learning almost by accident how to shoot ... all unsupervised.

One afternoon, I must have been about 8, Grandma Larson hailed me in as I was walking past her house. And pointed out a rabbit in back right underneath the apple tree.

We all knew saving the apples was important. Grandpa Larson sold them at a farm stand in the fall and family depended on them. He was meticulous about protecting and caring for his orchard. The rabbits did a great deal of damage, chewing the bark off young trees, ringing them so they'd die. She asked me to shoot the rabbit because none of the boys were home.

I puffed with boyish pride at being summoned to do man's job. It was a request of magnitude to be asked to protect their homestead and livelihood. I shot ... and missed.

The rabbit ran away. I stood embarrassed. My moment of glory would have to wait for another day. But that only whetted my appetite.

I practiced shooting with the BB gun every chance I got and by the age 12 everybody felt I was ready to receive Grandpa Ben's shot gun.

My grandfather had been known throughout the county as the best shot around and would take on anyone who bet they could outshoot him. The gun was a perfect fit for him and because I had a similar stature it was a perfect fit for me.

The gun was the stuff of family legend. It was the gun my grandfather had used on the Armistice day hunt November 11, 1940. Uncle Ted and Grandfather Ben went duck hunting on Lawrence lake north of Brownsville. It was warm for November—in the 60s—and no one had dressed for cold weather. Because of the high temperatures, duck hunting had been slow. Many people in that area depended upon wild game for their protein needs and duck hunting was a good way of filling up the freezer.

The northern flight hadn't come down yet from Canada and local ducks had already departed. Yet it was one of the last days of hunting season, so hunters descended upon the back waters of the Mississippi that day for the last hunt of the season. To many it turned out to be their very last day.

Initially only a few ducks were flying in the early morning and then the wind picked up and temperature started to drop. The mythical northern flight, pushed by the storm, descended upon the area, and ducks filled the sky. They were flying low and readily decoyed in. The limit was 10 ducks per person back then. Ted and Grandfather were captivated. They almost were filled out ... just a couple more to go. But it started to rain, then snow, and then the winds picked up gusting as high as 50 to 80 miles per hour. Grandpa's gun barrel was hot from all the shooting. But they couldn't bring themselves to leave such fantastic once-in-a-lifetime action. They held out until the storm developed into a blizzard.

Finally Grandpa said, "Let's go."

Ted threw the decoys in the boat and tried to launch it into the howling gale. The wind flipped it over and blew it right back onto the island upside down.

Ted panic and screamed they were going to die. He lamented that they stayed for the last few ducks. In his hysteria he shouted that they would freeze to death.

Grandpa slapped him in the face to calm him down.

And told him they would start a fire and wait until it blows over. But Ted raged. The wood was wet, the wind was howling. They were doomed.

Grandpa pointed to a huge drift wood stump that had washed down from previous floods.

And told Ted to get the gas can and pour it on … to make sure it lit from below, so the wind wouldn't blow it out. He had to shout to be heard over the gale.

Ted got the stump burning. It offered some shelter from the wind and the fire kept on burning for the next 48 hours. Ted was so cold that he trembled unable keep warm. Grandpa had him take the canvas decoy sack, cut it open to a more usable shape and sit under it on the burning stump in a spot where the heat and smoke came up, but the flames didn't burn him. Afterwards his eyes were so smoke filled that he couldn't see for three days.

They spent two nights out on the island on top of the burning stump. They ate roasted duck. It wasn't like the fare back home, but if you have nothing else to eat, duck roasted on a burning stump tastes surprisingly good.

Throughout the storm, Grandpa kept on shooting three rounds from that old shotgun. It worked! Uncle Bud located them because of that shotgun and along with a friend managed to slide a boat across the frozen lake and through snow drifts as high as 20 feet in places.

One hundred and forty-five people died from the storm. Most of them duck hunters on the Mississippi.

I had hunted since age 10 but only for pheasants, squirrels or cottontails, never for big game. During those hunts I used a borrowed single-shot 410 shotgun. Back then it was gun many kids learned to shoot with.

After my twelfth birthday, everyone agreed that I could go on a deer hunt when the season opened. This hunt was going to be different; we were going after deer and I had my own pump-action 12-gauge. My excitement for the upcoming hunt was so intense that I couldn't sleep at all the night before. It was the most significant event in my entire life … or so I thought.

It had snowed in the night, but the sun rose on a perfect mid-November morning. Uncle Ted drove us up to a small road off South Ridge west of LaCrescent. By the time we arrived it was light enough to see.

It was a prime spot for deer hunting, situated near the apple orchards. The local apple growers were continuously at war with the rabbits and the deer. The bucks destroyed the trees by rubbing their antlers against the young saplings. They also ate the tiny buds, and apples were one of their preferred foods.

Ted pulled over and my 13-year old cousin, Rich and I jumped out of the car and loaded our guns. Wooded hills sloped down from each side of the road. The sky was blue, and six inches of fresh snow sparkled with magical intensity. Ted said he had to go back into town to do something. (I think it was for a cup of coffee.). He would be back in an hour to see how we were doing.

We hadn't gone more than 20 yards into the woods when we found four sets of deer tracks in the fresh snow. We followed them not speaking, stepping lightly. The fresh snow muffled all sound and a gentle breeze blew the snow off the trees and bushes. We, of course, were on high alert as we made our way down a moderately steep slope covered with trees and brush. Each time a clump of snow fell, we tensed thinking it might be the deer.

The tracks told us that the deer were moving slowly, nibbling the tender tips of the small aspen saplings. We were on the trail for 20 minutes when a fat doe jumped up from her bed amongst the young trees and bramble bushes.

Rich shot first and incredibly missed. He was a good shot who had spent hours and hours practicing at shooting at clay pigeons. I, on the other hand, didn't have enough extra money to pay for shells or clay pigeons to practice. Nevertheless, I shot, but didn't notice any sign of wounding. The doe ran at a right angle to us and in about three bounds was out of sight in the underbrush. There was no chance for another shot.

It was dead silent—the quiet of winter in the north woods. The shots and the encounter seemed as loud as the finale of a grand orchestra, but it was only in my mind. My first shot at a deer got my adrenaline running. I was so excited. Just taking the shot—and so soon after the hunt began—was something even experienced hunters couldn't expect.

I knew from my encyclopedia on hunting, "Field and Stream," that we had to find the doe's trail to check her for injury. The snow made it easy to find her tracks … and a little blood! Fifty yards further we found her dead … a beautiful animal. Fresh red blood contrasted with the pure sparkling snow. I had made a good and fatal shot…my first shot.

I had never seen anyone gut a deer, but of course I knew exactly how to do it because of all the stories I had read in my "encyclopedia". But it looked like it was going to be messy, so Cousin Rich suggested that I keep my cotton gloves on and avoid getting blood on my delicate hands. Mind you he had never been deer hunting before and had never seen anyone field dress a deer. I didn't know if I should do it that way, but he was older, and I deferred to his greater knowledge.

We could have waited for Uncle Ted to do the gutting, but it was my kill and I wanted to rise to the responsibility. Uncle Ted always had us do the skinning and gutting of smaller animals we had hunted before. It is a man's duty to dress his kill. The night before I had sharpened my knife for the umpteenth time in anticipation.

I put my two fingers in a V-shape lifting the skin and cut carefully between them up the belly to the point where the ribs come together taking care not to puncture the organs. Some hunters cut through the sternum, but I didn't have the skill or physical strength.

My gloves and the sleeves of my jacket were covered in blood. I cut the pericardium, reached in the chest cavity, cut the heart free and yanked. The heart, lungs and intestines swished out onto the bloody snow.

We started dragging the deer up the hill to the road on the ridge. Snow made the dragging easier, but we were amazed at how hard it was going uphill. The deer was heavier than I had anticipated or maybe it was just because I was 12 years old and had no previous experience dragging out a deer. We pulled her up to the ditch by the edge of the road to await Uncle Ted. The snow was just deep enough so you couldn't really see her unless you were standing right above. Ten minutes later, Ted showed up.

He asked how the hunting was in a voice that let us know he knew we wouldn't have seen anything.

I answered, "Good. I got one." My voice was filled with pride. He didn't believe me and asked where it was. We told him it was 20 feet up the road in the left-hand ditch. Ted jumped out of the car and walked up the 20 feet and looked down on our kill. "Well, I'll be," he said shaking his head. At that moment I knew I had become a man … a real hunter.

Ted tied the deer to the roof of the car and we drove back to town. First, we had to stop at the house to show Aunt Miriam and then through town on a round-about route to the locker where the locals took their deer to be cut up and packaged. Ted made sure that everyone on the street saw our trophy. He was proud, and I was even prouder. But we still had one more day of deer hunting before I had to return to school.

I went to a suburban school that didn't recognize deer hunting as a legitimate absence. In northern Minnesota, school kids could take a whole week off for deer hunting. How I wished I was living and hunting in those zones … a place where the adults recognized the importance and necessity for such an endeavor. But alas, I had only one more day of hunting. I fell asleep that night thinking that just maybe, I might get lucky again!

Sunday came along with another clear blue sky and Ted drove us around on the small roads with woods and brushy thickets that looked like great deer habitat. I was frustrated because as he drove he kept up a constant stream of stories about seeing a deer here or there within the last couple of years, but he never stopped the car so we could get out and hunt.

The truth was he didn't really like to walk, preferring the comfort of the heated car with a radio so he could listen to the football games. We spent all morning driving and wasting time on the second day of my first deer hunt of my life looking for deer out the window. I was sure that it wasn't going to work when he decided to take the Hokah-Brownsville Road.

As we descended into the Brownsville valley, lo and behold, I spotted a deer standing 30 yards off the road in the woods looking at us.

Ted threw on the brakes. We slid a bit on the snow-packed, icy road. Cousin Rich was bound and determined to equal the hunt and wanted to take the sure shot out the window. In those days there was very little traffic and such violations were considered minor infractions.

He rolled down the window, shot, and missed. The deer bolted up the hill for 30 feet and stopped to look back at us. In the meantime, I had readied my gun just in case he missed again. When he did, I leaped out of the car, ran to the edge of the woods, took careful aim, shot and dropped the deer. I was elated! I ran up the hill and got within 10 feet of the deer when it stood up and started to run off. I shot again and down he went.

When Ted and Rich finally made it up the hill to my kill site, we looked for the two bullet holes but found only one through the body. The first shot had hit the deer on the right antler and had knocked it cold, but it wasn't a killing shot. Fortunately, because I had run up the wooded hillside after my first shot I was close enough to make the final fatal shot.

Again, I heard the trumpets and the grand march of the Toreadors … at least in my mind. I had scored … two deer in two days. Who was the man? I … the 12-year old, on his first deer hunt. What an unbelievable end for a first weekend of deer hunting. It was a true rite of passage.

I attributed my hunting success to my ability to spot wild game that others couldn't see. The deer's coat and color blended into the dark wood of the forest, at least to my hunting buddies, but not to me. I came to accept this vision as a natural gift. In fact, Ted and his sons hunted for a dozen years after this hunt before shooting a deer, even though they were expert marksmen. They could outshoot me when it came to duck hunting or skeet shooting, but when it came to "real" woods hunting, they never saw the deer or if they saw one, it was always too fast or too far away. I continued to hunt with them for several years and always shot deer for the hunting party and myself. I was recognized as the deer slayer. I was proud of the accolades I received from friends and relatives.

Years later I traded my grandfather's gun for a newer one and started missing shots I wouldn't have missed before. Eventually I adapted to my upgrade, but I wondered if there was some magic associated with my grandfather's gun, which had arrived in my life at the perfect time—a few weeks before my first deer hunt.

Six Poems
Robert Wooten

Last Days of Laissez Faire

They came up out of the creek
beside the road,
which turned into an abandoned car dealership
with an active snack machine,
one of the older models
still without a guard
to keep thieves from reaching up into it.
Raymond watched for John.
And then, they cut across a construction site
through a field of flying grasshoppers,
taking turns holding the bucket of turtles
and eating Bugles,
till they came to a wall of forest.
Here, they usually either stopped, went straight through
or turned aside,
depending on the way John chose
to make a subject of the secret marijuana,
growing in a clearing.

As Eric Clapton Is God

One Sunday morning,
Raymond found Dill outside.
"Why are you in the bushes?"
asked Raymond.

"Do you like 'Cocaine'"?
Dill asked, and blanched.
Raymond said he didn't know.
"It's a song," Dill replied.

Lightning

Raymond again wanted to learn Kung Fu.
Though once inferior to him
in fighting ability, the neighbor, T.,
now carried Chinese throwing stars,
nunchucks and a switchblade.
"I could defend myself from bullies,"
he told his Mom. One afternoon,
she left him at the Karate International.

They were all wearing belts and uniforms,
and Raymond thought they were going to give him one,
but they all had to do exercises, first,
and then, he was given laps to run.
He spent most of the evening watching it rain.

Bi-location

The ability to appear in two places at once,
'bi-location,' is considered a sign of sainthood.

And, after I had found my defrosted life totally thawed,
ready-to-go, I rose, at first, like fog, and then, as smoke,
into the vapor of the stratosphere
with angels in my ears, singing,
and the joy of life, throbbing in my veins,
and, with a smile, my ears still ringing.
I heard the formerly straight-jacketed man beside me
say, "Hah!" And then, he rolled his eyes.
In the deeps of angelic space,
I found a heavenly vehicle with keys, waiting.
It purred as the valet attendants snored who,
by drifting off to sleep here, (hah!) had missed me.
And yet, I exorcised myself of demons
by blasting off into space.

Later in that day on earth,
or in the mid-morning heat,
eyes found me in my death to the ward.
And, beyond the mist, through which, still, I could see
my slack limbs hanging at my side,
I shattered the cosmic record

for joyful overdrive. Once there,
my rhythm's sound carried beyond the other dead,
into the high blue earth sky, and across the minds
of puzzled people. And yet it is strained,
continually, over Dorothea Dix and into the wards,
where my warbling lifts the down-
cast hearts of rubber minds that
bounced against iron walls, seeking the final release.

A Counter-transference

 Everything's backwards, nothing's what it seems,
and nothing haunts my dream.
I no longer dream
at night, but I wake
to a world underwater.

Nothing is what it seems, nothing is real.
I'm reacting not to what I see
but to what I think and feel.
And I'm always "right this way."

Although my mind says
you're an obstacle in my way,
I know you
through your
feelings: "How are you today?" I ask,

as you're as everybody else—
and I believe you—"okay"—
no matter what my thoughts may say.

Reverse Psychology

It can't distinguish between a work of genius
and a genius at work, and keeps implying
it hears to people it can't imply know,
and saying to people it can't imply hear.

Who is this
that follows the day?

Come as a new economic
trend or clouds
before the cloudy
rainy cold day?
Sometimes, winter caught me
in the exuberance of spring.
Sometimes, the coldness
gripped me as I frolicked in the
rose gardens of my lifetime.
When did you get in?
How did you arrive?
The evening has come.
Have we been formally introduced?

Oh, the lion of winter,
you of frosty temper,
cold as breakfast
the day after,
sure as the ice on the
pond,
frost on the
    field.

You have bought stock in my life.
Take the shelter.
You can have the bedroom in back.
Take the stock.

AND what a rude one you are!
What of Spring and Summer?
I mean, what will they think?

If you are having a difficult time,
we hope that things will get better.

Sometimes, the coldness comes too quickly.
The withdrawal is begun.
I shall wave to the receding dulcet waters.
I shall have to sell my futures.

Call me if you get in.
They take the book.
Take care.

Lawn Adventures
Steve Cooke

*T*hat old house on Boston Street had quite a yard. You'd know the house if you saw it, with the curvy, ivy-shrouded front driveway and the rocks on the roof. The house itself wasn't much to look at from the outside, but it was where our family always managed to gather for holidays, birthdays, and any other time we just felt like getting together. I drove by it once, later on, after the family had grown old and things changed, but it just didn't look the same anymore. The current owner had even killed all the ivy. I will bet he found a few of my toys in there, especially the G.I. Joe's with the Kung-Fu grip.

My favorite place was always the back yard. Magic could happen there, and to a seven-year-old boy, it frequently did. An adult probably wouldn't see too much. He could quickly pace the length in twenty or thirty fast strides and go back along the width in half as many steps.

There was a birdbath in the far corner, but I never really saw any birds use it for bathing. I thought the ugly statue in the middle probably scared them away. They did like the feeders that were sitting, squatting, and hanging around the place. My granddaddy always made sure they were full of that red juice, seeds, and anything else he could put there. He knew all the bird names, and said he could even tell their mood, by the tunes they were whistling. He sometimes would whistle back with a different tune for each bird, but mostly we watched. My granddaddy liked them all, except for the pigeons. He had something against the pigeons.

He also had a little corner of Hawaii in that yard, snuggled up close to the house, where he could see it from his bedroom, and smell the flowers through the window. The star of that show was the Hibiscus plant with the big red flowers. It was nestled in with some ferns and other fancy plants. Granddaddy would always know their name too, but I could just remember the pretty ones. I once asked him once how the Hawaii plants could grow in California, and he said it was because of the trolls. He even showed them to me. Sure enough, there were two or three little green and brown men tending to the garden. I said they looked like statues and told him they couldn't be real, because they were so small, and didn't move. Granddaddy said they didn't move because they were afraid of people. He also said that if you were really quiet and sneaky, you could catch them at their gardening. We tried to sit on his patio and wait for them to start their gardening. I could never catch them at it. I always managed to move before they did. He always saw them move. He even knew their names somehow.

The best day came around once a week, but it always felt longer. I think it was Thursdays, but it's hard to be sure, it was way too many years ago. The first step was to get "geared up." For me, that meant getting to wear my special hat. It was big and round and white, with a wide, sturdy brim. Granddaddy had spocked the top with a bright red blot of paint to tease the hummingbirds. I found later that grown-ups would call it a Pith Helmet, but it was my safari hat. Wearing it meant we were going on an adventure.

While I was settling the hat on my head, making sure my laces were tied up real tight, and getting myself in order, granddaddy would wheel the electric chariot out of its home in the garage and get the long orange cord off its hook on the wall. His garage was always lined up just so, with a box or hook for everything and everything in its place. He always said he got in the habit way back when he was on the Battleships and never got out of the habit. He even had room in the garage to park his car there. Except for him, I had never seen anybody else park his car in a house. I thought that was what driveways were for. The garage at my house was so full, boxes would fall out if you tried to open the door. We didn't go in there much.

With the cord wrapped over one shoulder like a belt full of bullets, he would lead the mower through the gate and head for the back yard, with me running behind him. Once we got back to the lawn, there would always be some discussion about which way we were going to cut it. Sometimes we would start on the left, other times we would start on the right. Back-and-forth was okay, but you couldn't walk very far. One time, we even went round in circles, just to try it. Granddaddy rarely told me know when I wanted to try something a new way.

Once we had settled on the direction, it was time to get things started. There was a special plug by the Hawaii garden, which we used just for the mower. He always kept the blade sharpened just so. There was one time when he was putting an edge on the blade and the stone slipped, cutting his finger very deep. I heard some words that day that I had not heard before.

We would push that old electric owner from one end of the yard to the other, flipping the handle over after each trip. Sometimes we were in deepest Africa on safari looking for lost elephants. Other times we were down under (At that age I did not understand what we were under) chasing Aboriginals through the Outback. One time I asked him what they would be called if we were chasing them in the front yard. He just smiled.

One of my favorite adventures was the time when that magic back yard was the jungle of an Island in the Pacific. We were a patrol from the "Mighty Mo" hunting for enemy soldiers ready to jab us with sticks or make us eat raw fish. Granddaddy did not talk about his time on the big ships much, but when he did, the stories were usually worth listening to.

Flash forward about forty-odd years. I am the Grandpa now. Grandson is waiting out front for me to bring My magic chariot out. It is winter and the lawn is covered with Nebraska snow. The old trusty electric mower is long gone, probably sold at some garage sale in the distant past. My machine is a rechargeable snow blower with all the trimmings.

Yesterday we spent the afternoon down in the basement. I had piled some furniture up and covered it with blankets. This was one of his favorite pastimes. We would usually sit in his "fort" and read stories. Sometimes we would lay on the top of the tables and watch a cartoon, or old western. He has learned to love the sound of the William Tell overture, just like I do. His favorite was when we "built" a pirate ship. I found an old picture of a Jolly Rodger and taped it to a floor lamp. We stuck plastic sabers in our belts and wore old neckties tied around our heads.

I turn the corner and he is there by the porch waiting for me. Heavy jacket, full mittens, head fully covered by a woven ski hat, but somehow I can still see the huge smile he seems to always have when he visits. He wants to know if we can build a snowman like the last time. Sadly, there is hardly enough snow to cover the grass. I would probably not have bother clearing the walks, but he always gets such a kick out of pushing the blower. He is very careful and knows just how to work it. In some ways he is even better than I am with some things. It outweighs him by at least double, but he always manages to keep it running straight and true, even without my help. With all the clothing on, it is hard to talk, so I am content to just walk beside him. From comments I sometimes hear over the sound of the blowing snow, I know that he is sometimes a Transformer looking for Decepticons, Batman looking for the Joker, or one of the P.J. Masks looking for adventure.

He loves to play games, but we will not usually play by the normal rules. Sometimes it can be more fun to play by your own rules anyhow. It is not much fun to play Scrabble with a five-year-old that can barely read, much less spell high-scoring words. Instead, you use the tiles to build castles and fences and the Scrabble board becomes a fairy tale in the making. Almost any standard board game can become an adventure with a little creativity.

It is amazing to me still how getting out a couple of old cowboy hats or an old bedsheet and towels can transform even the most boring of rooms into a special place, but with a little bit of imagination, just about anything is possible. I think that is one of the best things about being somebody's Grandpa—you get to make the impossible possible and open the door to the wonderful world of make believe.

Eighty Days
Michael Ceraolo

Excerpt from "Eighty Days," which begin on July 2, 1881 when President James A. Garfield was shot by Charles J. Guiteau and continue through September 19, 1881 when Garfield died. Guiteau was later convicted of murder and executed.

July 19, 1881

Garfield:
What with my wounds
being described in graphic detail,
and the talk of my constant cheerfulness,
"I should think the public would be tired
of having me dished up to them in this way"

Guiteau:
"I thought the Deity and I had done it"

July 29, 1881

Garfield:
The members of the cabinet
came today to the Executive Mansion
for a cabinet meeting held at my bedside
This being summer,
there wasn't much for them to report,
but I still got the sense
they weren't telling me all that is going on,
possibly on doctor's orders

Guiteau:
I originally believed the choice
of Blaine as Garfield's premier
was an excellent choice

But when he told me
never to speak to him
about the job I sought,
or about any other job,

or about anything ever again,
I decided he was a "wicked man"
and that Garfield would have "no peace"

August 3, 1881

Garfield:
"I am a poor hater"

Guiteau:
"I had no ill-will to the President"

August 10, 1881

Garfield:
Today
I signed an extradition paper,
honoring Canada's request to return
a forger to our neighbor to the north
It was the first piece of official business
I've transacted since the shooting,
the re-beginning of the rest of my term

Guiteau:
"I think the American people
may sometime consider themselves
under great obligations to me"

August 22, 1881

Garfield:
"The truth will set you free,
                              but
first it will make you miserable"

Guiteau:
"I spit upon such evidence"
that there is any insanity
anywhere in my family

August 29, 1881

Garfield:
The doctors made an incision
on the right side of my face for pus drainage
Thankfully,
there are no mirrors close at hand

Guiteau:
"Be sure you get
the right expression of my face and eyes"
"I don't want to appear strained and awkward"

Burnt Potatoes
Roger McKnight

B&W from a photo by Anton Darius, unsplash.com

Rolf Quello was so set on some tasty carcinogens he didn't see the blonde woman in designer eyeglasses till they collided outside Al's Breakfast. Once inside, the two stood awkwardly together waiting for separate seats. When a lone customer got up by the window, they eyed each other until Rolf dashed the length of the diner and grabbed the spot for himself. Embarrassed at his own rudeness, he leaned forward pretending to study the menu, as she quietly took a now empty seat beside him and ordered two coffees. "One for him, too," she told the waiter.

Behind her words, Rolf detected a wry smile, so he went ahead and ordered himself the same breakfast as every Tuesday. "#2, over easy, bacon and hash browns." He didn't object when Al, the owner, patiently took the menu from him and placed it back in the counter rack.

Al repeated Rolf's order to the cook. "And burnt black."

"Sorry about my behavior," Rolf apologized to the young woman, as Al offered refills along the counter. "I'm famished, you know."

"Late night or early morning?" she asked.

"Both."

"Doing what?"

"Proofreading, copy editing," Rolf answered. "At a neighborhood newspaper. All night, every Monday. For free."

When the #2 came, he attacked the hashed browns with vigor, but after a few bites he turned and thanked her abashedly for the coffee, hoping this second apology didn't sound like an even worse afterthought than the first.

"Meg," she replied extending a hand, which he shook, noting how firm her grip was. "Margareta in full. Margareta Gradén. You know, *e* with an accent."

"Rolf here."

"That name! You're Swedish, like me!" she exclaimed and removed the Silhouette glasses to mark her surprise. The square rimless frame had made her visage seem angular and coldly professional, like her handshake, but without the glasses she showed a kind, mellow look, her cheeks soft, her eyes a light blue. "And you hell-bent on cancer? Ugh."

"Only one day a week," Rolf answered with a chuckle. He watched her until a happy glint showed in her eye. He finished the bacon and eggs, and Al came with a refill, so he sipped at the warm dark brew while listening to Meg, who added cream to her cup.

"I was born here in Minnesota but have lived all over," she explained. "Never abroad. You, though, intriguing. You add those burnt potatoes to top off the acid prose you correct all night?" She tucked the glasses away in her purse.

Rolf considered a clever reply but decided against bantering away his morning hours. He had another job to get to this afternoon and needed at least an hour's catnap between now and then. Still, he remembered having had a vague feeling someone was tagging behind him out on the sidewalk, and now in the café Meg's manner suggested a mixture of sly mischief and careful reserve. Her erect stance while waiting for a seat and now the firm outline of her breasts under a cotton blouse aroused a visceral sensation. Had she chosen him, while passing on the street, as a likely candidate? If so, for what? Sex and romance? Or talk?

"Something surely. But what then?" he asked, mostly to himself.

"At least it won't be today," she answered reflecting the vagueness of his question. "You can't develop cancer in a day, it takes years. But what about you, are you from there?"

"What? The old country, as they call it?" he asked with a serious look, squelching his visceral response to her. "Yes, in fact, but only sort of. My folks came here from Gothenburg, as a young couple, to sell import Volvos. Mom was already pregnant, so I was born in the U. S., but got this Swede name, fits my reticence, they say." Her question was a clear invite for him to ask about her, but instead it caused him to look back on his own origins, more than he was accustomed to, which brought on his serious expression. "As a child I spent summers at my grandparents' country cottages in Bohuslän. It was great fun, but as a youth I got wound up in the urban scene here and refused to go back across the pond. The excitement was here in Uptown, and I felt the beat, guess you might say. Then my parents were killed, in a boating accident on the St. Croix River. After that my interest in their homeland and Uptown faded, pretty much together."

He looked at Meg and wondered if she'd been listening. She was forming her lips in a circle, "Bo…"

"Bohuslän," he helped her. "It's an area around Gothenburg. I went to their funeral there, but I've never been back to visit the graves. Before they died, they had got to feel like strangers to me, money grubbing. 'The welfare state. You can't get rich in Sweden any more, they'd tell people, that's why we came to the States,' but I was already heading another direction. Psychology. Civil rights. LGBT. That stuff. I write an advice column for urban youth, the gender-bent mainly, along with proofreading."

"My dad's family came from Sweden, too," Meg announced. "South of Stockholm. They weren't farmers, like the rest who arrived here in the old days. Dad went to college to be a doctor but became a Lutheran pastor. We moved from church to church. I once went to eight schools in seven years. You straight? Married?"

Rolf shook his head no. "Was. Once. Married, I mean." He stopped himself from telling her about that youthful passion, which ended in disaster, but, thankfully, with no children. His ex-wife had gone on to trade in grain and cattle futures on the Kansas City market. She's like a man, his friends had said of her, but she was in reality the most feminine of women. Their marriage had ended more in dissonance over political views than long, drawn-out confrontations. He had since met other women, some of whom tantalizingly popped up online. He reacted in disappointment when their profiles failed to match their present status, which caused him to wonder in turn if he had unintentionally been been misleading in his own self-descriptions. With other ladies he had formed lasting friendships but experienced none of the chemistry so much ballyhooed on dating sites.

When he looked up at Meg, she was smiling, more through him than at him, or so he felt. He had noticed the same smile when she ordered coffee for them, as though she had been holding her next comment at the ready long before she uttered it. "I'm very good at guessing other people's ages," she began.

Rolf saw her focusing on his slightly graying temples, which he was sure she had noticed from the first but was re-evaluating now. He figured she would guess 42. He himself had never bothered greatly about how people showed their age. He reckoned any grown-up, say 25 or above, had to be his peer, or, in the work place, an equal colleague, an assumption he sometimes came to rue. Nevertheless, he expected Meg at any moment to place him in a firm category based on his perceived virility, insightfulness, or plain old listening skills. He wondered if she judged all men this way, and, if so, why.

"But nobody can guess mine," she continued, to his surprise. "I'm 32, but I can easily pass for 23." She put this out assertively, indicating she not only could but did move comfortably in different age groups.

"Sounds like an anagram. Transposing the 3 and the 2?"

"But I can do it," she protested.

"And you do, too? I mean, get confused for a 23-year-old?" Rolf asked.

"Most always," she said with pride.

We should all be so lucky, he started to say, but her words and attitude beat him to the comment, which felt just as well, given the cynicism, albeit gentle, imbedded in his own mixed memories of being that age. Instead he concentrated on Meg's looks. They were softly exceptional, punctuated by her smile, which actually seemed only a half-smile promising untold depths of love and empathy beneath the surface. Yet only time might tell whether physical and mental beauty would meld into unison in her case.

Whatever the scenario, her physical attractiveness was likely to grow stronger over time. He wasn't certain whether to tell her that, so he took the indirect path by sticking to anagrams. "Reminds me of George Orwell's *1984*. I read he wrote the book as an allegory about the horrors of Post-War Europe in 1948, so he switched the 4 and the 8, to 84. He had a reason, to avoid being deemed too blatantly critical of controversial issues in his own time."

Meg stopped to sip her coffee. Realizing it had grown cold, she stirred it vigorously to remix the coffee and cream, and then emptied the cup with a single swallow. "And you're guessing that approach applies to me? Skipping around, concealing my issues?" she asked.

"I don't know your issues," Rolf admitted.

Watching her placing the cup back down, he noticed her careful attention to detail combined with a slight twitch of the lips, suggesting a sense of vulnerability not noticeable in her previous all-so-knowing glance. He wondered if his intellectualizing about Orwell unnerved her or if she had been preparing to approach him about topics she had never discussed with a stranger before, or perhaps with no one, period, and he had foreseen where she was heading and beat her to the punch.

"With me it's all about love," she said. "Love. Every time I get in a relationship that makes me happy I feel I'm moving ahead in life, am giving something to the world and my partner. I want to accomplish something. Seventh heaven and all that. But when it fails, I'm crushed. I just want to leave."

"When it fails? Not if?" Rolf asked.

"It's never if, always when. When that happens, I want to get out of wherever I'm living and move off somewhere else. Blow this pop stand."

"Once and for all?"

"Yes, like in that old movie, *Charlie Bubbles*. Albert Finney, you know?"

Rolf shook his head no. "Tell me," he urged her.

"It's from way back, the sixties, saw it on a movie channel. Charlie Bubbles is a sales rep in England or somewhere, divorced, at a loss in life. One day a hot air balloon lands in a field and Charlie shrugs and climbs aboard and floats off with it, like on a cloud, out into the blue, away from his ex, his job, even leaves his kids. I've been on lots of hot air balloons. Moved around. L. A., then Philly, Boston, western Mass, Dallas, Chicago last."

"And so now back here? Your folks, whadda they say?"

"Nothing like yours would. They're not materialists. They never give me any of that go-get-a-job junk. Dad coulda made big bucks in medicine but chose the clergy. He says all a doc can do is keep you from dying. Pastors can help you find life."

"So why come back here?"

"To make something of myself. Maybe?"

"Trying to move ahead in life, without love?"

"With or without. I'm going to the U."

"To do what? The clergy? Like your dad? Save lives?"

Meg looked down and smiled demurely. "I've always dreamed of writing screenplays, but not like *Charlie Bubbles*. It's way too anti-climactic. The guy just flies off. I'm about love. Remember? Where do people find it? Where do I find it? How to keep it."

"And so, at present?"

"Love's on hold."

"But not failed?"

"How'd you know that?"

"Obvious, you don't seem to be fleeing."

She looked him straight in the eye as if to say this is serious, my life, I need to tell about it, but then she gazed around Al's tiny café, with its mingling of displaced street people, bright-eyed college students, and fond couples, all oblivious to the drama embroiling Meg's inner self. Rolf looked around with her. Out through the only window they could see workers rushing off on their daily business. Only Al---tall, lean, and unshaven---looked Rolf and Meg's way, offering them yet more coffee, which they refused, and seeming bemused by the human comedy. Rolf guessed conversations like theirs had played themselves out within his earshot untold times.

"I'm in a relationship now," she began. She took out her glasses and fiddled with them, but didn't put them on, which meant she chose against the businesswoman look.

With relish, Rolf attacked the last of his hash browns, now long since cold like Meg's coffee. Reduced by the flames to a charcoaly essence, they tasted delicious, even if experience and food science said they came up short on sustenance. After finishing the meal, he glanced up at Meg and said, with a slight tinge of impatience, "Go on."

"But it's on hold," she continued.

"Love, that is. Like you said?"

She nodded. "I was taking a course, The Modern Novel, and met this guy in class. Jamie. We start talking one day during break, kinda bump into each other, but not like you and me." She motioned toward the door and gave a wiggle like Rolf giving her a subtle bump, which he wondered if he actually had done at the entrance. "I mean with Jamie and me it was by design. We'd been eyeing each other for a while. His comments during class discussions were always out in left field, but interesting anyway, they caught my attention, like he thinks Hemingway was gay, so I totally laughed, but, you know, we started meeting private and he came up with passages from *For Whom the Bell Tolls* about a wounded soldier in an Army hospital, being cared for by this horny nurse, and the guy does it with her but he's latent, you get it, that kinda made sense to me."

"Latent homosexual, you mean?"

"Yeah, like, well, anyhow, fate or something led Jamie and me to each other out in the hallway during class break. When we were alone off campus, I kidded him about his ideas and then we started comparing notes for a paper we had due. By then we were reading Graham Greene and he said he was considering writing on guilt and the Catholic mind, which I thought was way-out whacko till he said he was Catholic and had once studied at a priest seminary. Had thought of spending his life hearing confessions and that. All these people's sins."

"And you'd never dated a Catholic before," Rolf surmised.

"Dated? Never really knew any."

"In all your 32 years, not even in Boston?"

"Well, maybe a few there, Irishmen, pub crawlers, but back at the pass. Not long and then we're dating. Jamie's so soft and caring, sensitive. Never been with a guy like that before, so I started thinking maybe *he* was gay, not Hemingway. But he gave the lie to that in a rush. I never been held like that before, not by anyone. We fell in love."

"Just what you're looking for. Why put it on hold?"

"Not me. Him. He's 24 and has someone back East, who lives there still. It's weeks before he tells me this."

Back East, Rolf thought. A guy or a girl? He decided it didn't matter, though something must have bothered this Jamie. "No one stops a mad love affair in mid-stream, no matter what they've got back East," Rolf said.

Meg thought his comment over but waved her hand as if it was off-base.

"Before long Jamie decided he needed more time to think things over. Now I haven't seen him forever."

"Which is how long, in the real world?"

"A month-and-a-half."

"So you're thinking of leaving again?"

"No, but I'm eight years older than him and women mature faster. We were just doing college stuff. Still, he said he saw I had developed faster. He couldn't get over it, how advanced I was."

"Of course, what did you expect?" Rolf asked. Only natural, he thought to himself, considering your age, but he stopped when an alternative occurred to him. "So you lied to him? About your age?"

"Twenty-three's only a year younger than him," she replied.

"And Jamie thought you'd lived in all those different cities and were still college-age?"

"He said he wanted more time. I could live with that. He said it with tears in his eyes, sitting on the edge of his bed one night. Bawling, can you believe it?"

"He never put the pieces together about you? And what about the other girl?"

"He never said."

"You never asked?"

Meg paused and wrinkled her brow as though she was trying to imagine a worthy rival for Jamie's affections.

"What did he tell you about her?"

"Maybe I wasn't listening."

Rolf glanced out around the café again. Breakfasters filtered out and joined the crowd of pedestrians passing Al's window. He wondered if Meg had some place to get to, like him, which made him think maybe they were not so unlike. She had possibly trailed him, Rolf, to the café and lived a lie with Jamie, the guy she professed to love, but Rolf himself had acted rudely to her and never been stunningly successful with romance in his own right. She runs from relationships, he reflected, while I bury myself in work to avoid starting them.

"Maybe I wasn't listening to what he said," she repeated. "I don't remember. I chose to forget probably."

If the love interest back East was a her, Rolf thought. He motioned to Meg that he had to leave and took the check from Al. "Coffee's on me," he said. He paid at the till before opening the door for her.

"I'm parked down there," Rolf said out on the sidewalk. He pointed to a ramp.

"What I can't forget is the tears," she continued, walking by Rolf's side. "It wouldn't have been anything if he'd just said it straight out, how he realized I developed faster. But while crying? I still can't deal with it."

"Deal with what? Losing him?"

"No, the tears. He loves me."

"But he loves somebody else more?"

"Maybe."

The parking ramp was a block away, so Rolf asked if she needed a ride somewhere. There was still time for her to say yes. He wouldn't have minded. Not every day a lovely young woman singled him out, yet he needed a nap before his p. m. shift at County Hospital.

"Like I said, a man turning away like that and crying. I expected more. I don't need this in my life."

"Need what?"

"Being a loser. I don't want young people thinking, I'm just an old loser."

Look at me, Rolf wanted to reply. Unloved. Looking, but never finding. But you're a man, that's different, he knew that's how she'd answer and he saw the point.

He waited as his weariness began to take hold. "You know, you have to have a thing before you can lose it," he finally said.

A moment of doubt flitted across her face. "By my reckoning, I feel 20 years younger than you."

"Now maybe," he agreed, "but in a few years you'll know it's only ten."

"What else do you do that makes you so tired?" she asked. "Besides proofing and bad food."

"Listening to people's problems. I'm a resident psychologist," he chuckled.

"And you meet a weirdo like me on your morning off?" she answered with a feigned gasp that highlighted a twinkle in her eye.

A winning rejoinder failed him. This Meg could seduce any man she wanted, he knew, and then desperately wait to lose him. Just as she was about to lose Rolf's company now, and he hers.

"Thanks for prying all that info out of me," she said.

"What info is that?"

"You know."

She seemed to consider where her next sentence would lead, but she surrendered only a slight frown, letting the thought drift away, hot-air balloon-like and un-retrieved.

Even if he had experienced or heard about most behaviors, Rolf felt perplexed by a woman clearly unguarded in expressing her feelings, yet so apprehensive about where they would lead her.

"Remember Margareta Gradén," she said.

As she turned to go, Rolf wondered if they'd forget each other. He guessed he'd choose not to, but he only knew for sure he had to catch some sleep and work was waiting. As for Margareta Gradén, she disappeared among the downtown throngs, and he lacked the time to stay and watch.

Three Poems
Kay Bosgraaf

Onion Futures

If we needed a break we would walk to the edge
of the onion field to the old hand pump, prime it, cup
our hands and drink in the shade
of the willow tree. My twelve-year-old eyes saw
so many onions in a long day in the sun that at night
I dreamed about onions rolling in great streams
and waterfalls making me dizzy in my sleep.

Michigan onions are ripe for harvest
in August, acres of neat rows of gray-green
spikey tops waving in the hot wind to us cousins
to drop down on our knees, tug at a clump,
lift them from the rich black soil. Holding
a bunch in my left hand, I take my foot-long
shears and slice through the tops letting
the onion heads thump and bounce in the bottom
of a wooden crate whose slats are weathered gray
from years of being filled with onions over and over.
We four keep at it, the onions slowly piling up
rounding off the crates.

Earning ten cents a crate to spend at the county
fair, we ride the tilt-a-whirl, the Ferris wheel,
feel our stomachs in our throats, walk slowly
through the freak house, pluck at our pink cotton
candy, all to the exciting music of the merry-go-round
and the carneys shouting. We use the rest room
where a black woman sits on a chair with a bowl
of nickels and dimes on the counter in front of her.
Why is she there? My cousins don't know either.
At last we go our separate ways. Clutching my new
teddy bear, I walk home alone down the dark
country road past the onion fields lit by the moon
that casts my shadow beside me.

Dinner Alone at Ledo's

I hear a hollow thump and know that the father
in the next booth stuck his fist into one
of his three girls. Violent movies, solid hits
on the back have taught me this sound. After
the thump, I hear perfect silence and then a mournful
scream bursts from the toddler sitting next to him.
While she tries to catch her breath, he says, "I told you
not to stand up." She wanted to see
who was sitting behind her. "Be quiet. Stop crying.
I said, Stop crying now." She gasps for air
as she tries to still her sobs, tries to obey
him and finally quiets herself as her sisters
watch from across the table. "Sit up straight
in your seat," he says to another one. "Sit up
straight or we'll have to leave and I'll tell
your mother. Sit up straight." If dad uses
his fisted voice and hand, I wonder what mom
will use. Watching him on the sly since I sat
down in my booth, I wonder if one of the girls
when she is older will kill him in his sleep.
Soon he leaves with his three disheveled girls
lagging behind, one still clutching her slice.

Driving Home

At dark two police cars—red blue swirls
siren whorls— slide horizontally across
four lanes of traffic toward the chilly concrete
barrier—park before the old blue panel van
with sunken front end in cold November

in the red blue swirls
a dozen people in winter jackets
slouch around—traffic slows
an officer proceeds north on foot
along the concrete barrier

up the median gun glinting
in the headlights of eight lanes
from ahead and behind,
then the partner, gun in hand, follows backing him up
miasma of red, blue, white—the doe leads them

as fast as her percussive legs allow
up the highway median beside the gray chill barrier
two strong front legs haul her body
hobbled hind legs trail
in the strobe of red and blue swirls

one officer behind the other in their tan uniforms
her soft tan hide and thick white tail
she still leads with two legs dangling
hooves clack in their raggedy dance
joints and feet point this way and that

soon a pointed metallic sphere will breach her fur
echo off the barrier past
the cold red swirls
and into the waiting woods
as I slowly begin my drive up 270

Two Fish Tales

Jim Johnson
Emeritus Poet Laureate of Duluth, Minnesota

Old Brook Trout Guys

When I grew up fishing Northern Minnesota brook trout, I met a few old brook trout guys. Marvelous individualists, I thought. I even longed to be one of them. They were old war veterans, now widowed, no kids who ever visited. Perhaps never able to handle the technicalities of domestic life. Or never lucky enough to meet that special woman who would introduce him to the wonders of civilization. These men lived alone so far back in the north woods waiting for that knock on the door of his shack that he may have hoped was a woman as lonely as he was. But was usually some young trout bum, like I was, wanting to talk trout. Eager for trout wisdom.

Before one of these old men even opened the door, I was already longing for the ambiance of that rough-hewn cabin. Shelves of bags of sugar, salt, flour. Cans of beans and Arco coffee. On the oil cloth covered table a kerosene lantern. In a corner stacks of *Outdoor Life, Field and Stream* magazines, and other essential literature. In another corner, books, I was sure included *Moby Dick,* Thoreau, and Whitman, but too dust-covered to ascertain. And a pot of coffee always on the wood cook stove.

This was an old backwoodsman who might have lived his life as a logger until social security set him up on the banks of a Northern Minnesota trout stream with twenty acres, a shack, plenty of popple trees to cut for wood to feed the wood stove, a spring or pump for water, and an outhouse. What more could a man want? He had all winter to read and enough mosquitos to keep him company in the summer. He shot his deer in November and caught trout all summer.

This seemed to me to be the only life.

And each old man brook trout hero of my youth was happy, happy to see it me, even in his deafness and the greater deafness of the faithful dog at his side, pounding at his door.

Of course I wanted to pick his mind, add new possibilities to my list of streams, as he moved dirty plates and silverware to the sink to clear a place for me at the table, set a china cup with the handle broken off before me. He poured coffee cooked camp-style, handfuls of coffee dropped into a granite pot of fiercely boiling water, the coffee arcing down and with a quick lift of the pot and the final plop! into my cup. Then he pushed the depression glass bowl of sugar complete with a sugar-crusted spoon and the can of Carnation milk with two holes pegged with sticks towards me.

O to live like this forever.

As education is so often wasted on the youth, the days of my youth, I felt, were mostly wasted on education. Because of school I could only fish on weekends. In those days, if I fished on Saturday I had to be out early. If a car was parked in the pull-off by a stream, I drove to the next stream hoping no one would already be there. Then there were many good brook trout fishermen. Not all of them old. Then there were a lot of good brook trout streams. And a lot of brook trout.

Even then I had to walk, especially on Saturdays. The easy places were usually fished out, so a long walk could reward me with good fishing. Or not. Many winter nights were spent pouring over maps, planning assaults into new territories.

And there were many long days of walking--off trails, through the brush, by compass--walking in hot rubber hip boots, hat, flannel long-sleeved shirt through thick alder and hazel brush, around windfalls with deer flies at the back of my neck, only to find the stream of my dreams had no water. Or the beaver dam was blown out. Or I couldn't even find the stream. Then after not fishing, the long walk back, hoping not to get lost.

But. Sometimes.

I caught brook trout. Beautiful brook trout— dark olive vermicular-backed with red and blue spots haloed like stars, bellies red as sunset. Brook trout on every cast, though only six inches long. Or ten ten-inchers (the limit then was ten) in a creel filled with sweet fiddlehead ferns. Or maybe a twelve-inch fish-of-the-day. A fifteen or sixteen-incher would have been even in those days the fish of the season. These were the possibilities that drove me on.

I always searched for that elusive beaver dam or deep dark hole were the big trout lurked. I even found a few. But because beavers were trapped, roads built, trees logged, land sold, many these places are now gone. And there are fewer and fewer new possibilities. Now there are more roads, trails—hiking, snowmobile, cross country ski, ATV—and more cabins (vaulted-ceilinged mansions not shacks), more logging, mining, our technologically-driven need now for paper, copper, nickel.

Brook trout are small. I think they are even smaller now. There are fewer places for long walks without trails. The streams are warmer, logged right to the alder edge.

Brook trout are fewer.

And fishermen who fish for them are fewer.

Many of the fishermen once so eager to get out early on the Saturday pull-offs of my youth are gone, dead, or too old to walk the trails. Or maybe they are too wise to walk the bug-filled brush for the diminished possibility of a small, though beautiful, trout.

I could be the last Northern Minnesota brook trout fisherman, I thought when I bought my cabin near Isabella, Minnesota. I was married with kids, living in a city, so I could only steal a few days to fish each summer. Then one day, it was the day after Christmas, my wife told me to leave.

My former life, I knew, had been troubled. We tried counseling. When I tried to explain how I thought she didn't listen to me, she cut me off. The counselor suggested that maybe I had a point. After that she refused further counseling. I never knew how to talk about not being able to talk. Later I told my story to another counselor. To tell my story was healing so I don't need to tell that story now. I do need to tell you what became my life.

I left. I was lost in my thoughts.

The late December darkness lingered on through January and February. In March I noticed the longer days and warmer sun melted snow along the ridges. When I smelled the pine duff, I thought about brook trout. Then more snow fell in April. Finally, despite the black flies in May, the mosquitos in June, I went brook trout fishing.

I was alone then. I was at my cabin. I was at my shack with no one to talk to. There had been no long-term planning for this perimeter man, no end-of-the-road counseling, no hermits- without-television, or the sequel, hermits-without-internet. I was alone.

So I fished.

I fished brook trout all summer. I found old places, though many of these places were lost. But I also found new places--a deep beaver dam, a meandering spring creek, a fast water run dropping off into a deep hole beside a huge basalt boulder, a glacial erratic. And once again, I caught brook trout as beautiful as ever. Not as many. The limit now is five, though I only take one, like an osprey. And I never fish the same hole twice in a season.

That first summer I was back.

The second summer too.

The third summer I noticed there was no one to tell these stories to. I was writing. Though my stories all seemed to have a Roads-of-Lake-County ending.

Perhaps that was the destiny I believed in.

When you knocked on the door.

Not exactly. We had met at a poetry reading. You told me you were from Iowa and had vacationed in Ely. Then you asked me if I really lived in Ely, Minnesota.

I had to admit I lived in Isabella, Minnesota.

Then when you arrived with gray blond hair, Fay Dunaway lips smiling at my door, I told you my story. About how I could have been, not only an old brook trout guy, but the last living old brook trout guy in Northern Minnesota.

And you listened.

And because you listened, I had to listen to your story. I won't tell. I only want to say I am no longer alone though I still fish the new old brook trout places. When I do, I visit with those old brook trout guys. I see them along the streams, though they are ghosts as all memories ever are, like the wind in the cedar boughs or the trickle of a creek, telling me their secret places. I know one day I too will be one of them. But not yet.

Trout fishing In Iowa

The second day I fished in Iowa was on a Sunday, mid-October. The temperature 70 degrees. The sky was clear as trust. I drove a gravel road down a steep descent through shag bark hickory, black walnuts (an area where I have since seen pheasants, turkeys), crossed an iron bridge, and parked. Pulled on waders, vest and rigged my fly rod. Walked to a barbed wire fence with a sign: *Fishing Access. Respect private property.* Climbed the walkover and walked upstream. The stream was about as wide as my fly rod (I like a ten-foot rod with a soft to medium action) was long. It ran fast along a rock riprap, through a bed of watercress, and into a pool that deepened, slipped like a dream under the bridge and beyond, undercutting a rooted bank.

I cast my cast (old wet fly term) of two wet flies, a Royal Coachman as my solicitor and a Partridge and Olive as my point, to the far edge where the fast water tumbled into the darker depths, mended my line, and let the flies swing in a lifting arc to the top of the pool. Watched for rises.

Noticed the leaves falling were the colors of brown trout.

Another car crossed the bridge and parked. A man put on waders, fly vest and threaded a line through the guides while a woman gathered a wooden folding chair, hard cover book, book club choice perhaps, pushed her sunglasses up into her hair. Then they walked to the fence and over the walkover. The man stepped first to the top, then extended his hand to the woman to help her up and over. Then they walked up beyond me to the short grass green pasture. The woman set up her chair under an old oak, sat, opened her book, and looked out at the stream, her fisherman walking into position at the top of the run. The man's eyes slid over the water as his right hand holding the handle of the fly road rose quickly to slightly above his shoulder, and the fly line, leader, and fly flicked back and straightened out behind him, hung there for a moment and

I thought I was in the North Country of England. Or in Scotland. This setting was right out of Masterpiece Theater.

Another car, another man and woman arrived, carried lawn chairs, styrofoam bait box, spin rods and sat down below the bridge.

Then a Dodge Ram pickup with Leaping Brook Trout Iowa license plates pulled up. A man with a spin rod walked downstream. I know a man with a spin rod and spoons or Mepps spinners could cover a lot of water, make three or four casts in a hole, then walk to the next. He might hook a big brown trout. Or he might not. But a guy could.

This was a busy autumn day. The Hawkeyes had played on Saturday. People wanted to be out on Sunday. Yet I knew there would be a place for me as I walked the Department of Natural Resources trail upstream. This, I thought, was Iowa.

The first day I fished, or tried to fish, in Iowa was below the Decorah Fish Hatchery. I parked on the paved parking lot below the huge white pine with the large eagles' nest, then walked a paved path to the stream. An old man was seated on a folding stool beside the bridge watching the tip of his rod, the monofilament fish line that disappeared into the water below. I never saw him move.

Unlike the woman in bright red knee-high rubber boots who walked from the run that spilled out of the hatchery across the bridge to the other side, then downstream. She carried her white styrofoam bait box in one hand, her Zebco spin cast rod in the other. In each spot she cast two or three times and then moved briskly on then to the next.

A contrast in styles. These kind always pair up. The one who fishes one hole all day long. And the other who moves, wants to cast to every spot.

I left the stream to them. Not a cast.

I grew up fishing Montana. Where the rivers are larger--cold beautiful womanly rivers everyone could love--but now overcrowded with guides, drift boats, private lodges, purists, catch and release (only ospreys can keep trout).

Trout fishing for me is, always was: to walk, wear a big hat, carry a long rod, fish two wet flies. And to be alone. Except for the fields, trees, stream. Maybe an eagle. And my own thoughts. Maybe the possibility of a few rises. Or maybe not. That's fishing. That and solitude. Knowing the connection to the natural world (for me the fly rod, reel, line, leader, flies) is that awareness of the world within me is also outside of me. That the two are the same.

This is what I was thinking as I walked along the Iowa DNR trail. Though three other cars were parked by the bridge, I was alone.

I was trout fishing in democratic Iowa.

2000 years ago glaciers rolled over much of the Upper Midwest, but fell short in Northeast Iowa (as well as Southwest Wisconsin and Southeast Minnesota). Hence the name Driftless Area.

The runoff from those receding glaciers carved out valleys, left fertile loess on uplands, cut through porous sandstone, shale, dolomite, and limestone bedrock that soaked up moisture and created springs and coldwater flows

rich with alkaline, calcium

yielding insects, crustaceans

flowing through steep gradients

riffles, oxygenated rapids, as well as spring creeks

along limestone ridges covered with moss, filled with Paleozoic fossils.

Then the hills plowed, planted over.

And floods of mythological proportions washed away top soil, deposited silt.

In the 1930s the Civil Conservation Corp began erosion control. Since then the Iowa DNR, Trout Unlimited, and local landowners have worked together, not only to prevent erosion, but improve stream habitat, increase natural spawning, and provide angler access.

Now as I walked the two-rutted trail along a dried corn field on one side of me, the gospel gurgling, on the other, told me it was water.

Water flowing as rich as any English chalkstream.

In Iowa where I was now alone. Trout fishing. The same Iowa so many left for the dream we call The West.

I have heard it said that if the Yellowstone River is the Yankee Stadium of fly fishing, then the Bighorn River is Fenway Park. To that I would add: and the trout streams of Iowa are *A Field of Dreams*.

water & sand – Two Poems
Nicholle Ramsey
Associate Poet Laureate of Winona, Minnesota

sometimes

sometimes i sit on the bathtub floor,
naked, of course, let water run hot.
hit my face like an imitation drowning
or elsewhere rebirth. sometimes
i trace the spines of books as if i know
their whole story, superficial,
but sometimes the spine tells all
like a book read over and over again
his snakes, cowers, and curls. collapsible.
as if he is my copy of the little prince,
picking it up even though i know the ending.
sometimes i call because it's all my fingers
know to do. and we shoot shit. but sometimes
i call because sleepy dream souls
float down river, pinch me, please,
until i open my eyes again.
because sometimes i like to stare
into your eyes at sunrise. the warmth
of getting lost in green comforts,
but i am forgetting the whole forest
is behind you i hold your body by the roots, i pine.
and sometimes i run away to the back waters
of mississippi with only a pack of cigarettes,
let my toes prune in the river
and chain smoke until i am ready to go home.
sometimes i think you are my home,
my naïve childhood game of make believe,
my white picket fence, garden, loveseat,
weird art in the living room. my permanent.
and sometimes you have to wake me up, remind me
that you are not even my cardboard box
not for always, just sometimes.

the forgetful

my grandmother's stomach sinks
every time her husband
has a name,
a memory,
what he had for lunch
on the tip of his tongue.
never says it.
old enough to have thoughts
slip through his fingers.
like the sand of the michigan lake
that he and i visited years ago

i kiss him on his bald spot again,
always, as he sits in his lazy boy.
He trembles to asks me who i am
it's me, nickie.
he tells me i look like just like his wife when they met.
says i can't be nickie
shakes his head
 and he places his hand at a height i used to be,
just above his waist.
no, grandpa, i'm a little older than that.
old enough to understand
that from here on out I will just be a sepia tone photo from 1952,
just a reincarnation of his young wife.

he forgets the alphabet
gets silent half way through,
stares forward with a fading shine
and asks for my grandmother,
who laughs at his jokes,
she has heard them all before,
and her laughter will eventually turn to a quiet sob.
exhaustedly in love,
but in love nonetheless.
the gleam in her eyes painfully watches his eyes dull.
she old enough to understand
her husband is slowly walking away
while sitting in a lazy boy.

Feast & Requiem
By John Torgrimson

The Funeral Feast

Jamis stopped by our leaf hut at daybreak to invite me and Pat to his father's funeral feast. He was on his way to his bush garden to pick sweet potatoes and yams for the celebration.

The sun at dawn was muted, splayed across the horizon in a glow of amber, the nocturnal creatures still yelling and singing in the humid haze of the jungle. In an hour they would become silent with the rise of the sun, letting the parrots and cockatoos working the day shift take their turn at noise making.

"When did old Festus die?" I asked sleepily. The water was still hot in the kettle and I handed a cup of instant coffee, with great gobs of sweet and condensed milk, to Jamis.

It was not unusual for people to just up and die in the jungles of Guadalcanal—pneumonia, malaria, old age or a combination of maladies just too overwhelming for most

Photo by John Torgrimson

malnourished bodies to withstand. People were always saying, "Oh, it's just the flu – hacking and coughing, bundled in jackets and blankets in the 90-degree heat, until one day they would just slip away.

Or they would blame it on the Vele Man—a minute invisible voodoo sorcerer, with a tiny basket of black magic, who would cast spells on the innocent and not so innocent as they walked by. The Vele is fast and can circle the entire island in a second. He needs to see you before you see him in order to work his spells.

After three days with a fever, people would say, "Mai karange, Vele hem e kasem mi bigtaem." (My goodness, the Vele really got me.)

People that were sometimes on the outs with the tribe were often accused of being Veles or at least in cahoots with him. When you'd say that the storekeeper was too tall to be a Vele, they'd say that when he becomes a Vele he assumes a different form. They were convinced of this logic, and no religion was going to tell them otherwise. And so, blaming the Vele Man explained the unexplainable to those living this hard, short life.

The village chief's three-year-old son, a chubby little gremlin, who was always wondering around the village naked, died from malaria or the Vele depending on whom you talked to. His father took him to the doctor and to a medicine man on the off chance that one of them would come up with a cure. He was a cute little bugger.

And now Festus was dead. "Good God," I said to Jamis. "I didn't even know that your father was sick."

"He's not. And he's not dead either. Not, yet anyway," countered Jamis in an exasperated tone. "But he thinks he's going to and wants to have a feast before it's too late. I told him to wait awhile, but he insisted."

He stopped for a moment to sip his coffee and let this bit of coconut news sink in.

"I came by on my way to the garden to invite you," he went on. "My old man would be pleased if *ruka monesere* (the two white folks) would come."

Jamis was one of the villagers we liked most. Tall for a Solomon Islander, he was easy going and hardworking, certainly one of the leaders on the cacao project we were heading up as Peace Corps Volunteers. About six months into our two-year stint, we found ourselves at a culturally loss over Festus' funeral request and concluded there was much more we needed to learn about the ways of the people in our village. We told Jemis we would be honored to come.

My wife, Pat, and I were community development workers assigned to three resettlement villages on the north coast of Guadalcanal. The villagers had been displaced the previous year when an earthquake wiped out their villages and killed 11 people. The newly independent government had moved them from the weathercoast, on the windward side of the island, to Crown land about 20 miles from the capital, Honiara. Funding from Europe's Common Market was helping with their resettlement and supporting efforts for the villagers to adopt cash crop farming methods to replace the traditional slash and burn farming they were accustomed to. This is how we found ourselves living in a jungle village, developing a cacao plantation.

Of the more than 200 islands in the Solomon Islands chain, located between New Guinea and Fiji, Guadalcanal is one of the largest islands at 90 by 35 miles, with central mountains splitting the island down the length of it. Several battles in the Pacific during World War II took place on Guadalcanal or in its waters, colloquially known as Iron Bottom Sound due to the tonnage lying at the bottom of the sea. And 40 years later, visible remnants from the fighting dotted the shore line and unexploded ordnance rotted away in the jungles. Most people lived in remote villages, with small population centers on the islands and provincial centers.

Although Festus was a convert to the Anglican church, this practice of funeral feasts without a corpse was a customary rite handed down from tribal tradition. Most churches frowned on these old ways, but Festus was determined to follow the customs of his people. "The priest doesn't need to know," he would tell me later.

Traditionally, funerals were elaborate affairs, sometimes lasting several days. In the old days, they would bury a chief and other big men in the sitting position, a few inches under the ground's surface. And every day women from the village would pour water through a bamboo tube onto the head to encourage decomposition of the flesh around the skull. Eventually, the shrunken skull was detached from the body and placed in the Haus Tambu. This holy place was a memorial to the big men of the village and was a visible connection for the tribe to its ancestral past.

The custom of the funeral feast is about the passing of the torch to the next generation. In front of the entire community, Festus gave instructions to each of his children. To Jamis, he said: "This house, and the family that lives inside it, that which has been mine for all of these years, is now yours."

Festus reached into a brown satchel made out of pandanas leaf and pulled out some items. "I came into this world with nothing and I will leave with nothing," he said.

He handed some traditional shell money to Jamis. "This money has been in our family for a long time. It connects me to those before me. It connects me to those who come after me. And so, too, you will pass it on to others in our line."

The ceremony concluded with different people praising Festus. Many of the eulogies acknowledged his adherence to the old ways— "Man e blong kastom" was uttered more than once. A man who follows the old customs and traditions is held in high esteem in village society.

I wasn't prepared to say anything, content being a bystander at this event, but Jamis asked me if I would speak.

"Festus is a simple man, a hardworking man," I began, a bit unsure whether to use present or past tense since the deceased-to-be-was standing a few yards from me puffing on a pipe. "A man who always takes responsibility for his actions. He doesn't talk much, but when he does he always has something important to say and people listen. I have much respect for him."

Festus smiled and nodded his head in acknowledgement. This prompted me to add, "and I hope he lives to see several more grandchildren come into this world." To which Festus replied in Pidgin English, "Mi no save duim. Mi kolsup dae nao." (Can't do it; I'm close to dying now).

Requiem

Every afternoon, about five o'clock, when the sun has turned and the heat of the day is beginning to wane, about the time that 10,000 Vietnamese refugees have finished English classes for the day and are making the long march to their billets to fry their meager rations in chilies and garlic and fish sauce, at a time when the camp workers are heading to the Guest House to quaff their thirst on ice cold San Miguel at four pesos a bottle, Doug Ramsey emerges from the head office.

Tall and thin, his manners Quakerish, Ramsey is a solitary figure, his head slightly bent downward as he walks. He has a look of distraction as if he, and he alone, populates the world in which he lives in.

The feast was a grand party, with Festus presiding. Freshly killed pigs baked in an earthen oven alongside sweet potatoes, cassava, taro and yams, all served on banana leaves. The whole village turned out for the event, gorging themselves on the takings.

We saw Festus a few times after the party and he always looked happy and well. Then one day, about two months after the funeral feast, he died in his sleep. We didn't bother to ask what he died of. Old age, cancer, malaria—what difference did it make? There was no terminal diagnosis from a doctor in the capital, he just knew he was going to die and so he did.

He was buried on slightly descending grassland facing the Pacific Ocean. As funerals go, his was the most casual one I'd ever been to. No sniffling, no sobs, no keening. Just an Anglican priest, a few words of praise to God, and the sound of sand and gravel falling on a wooden box.

In life Festus was both illiterate and impoverished with few possessions. But from the time of his funeral feast, he was somehow able to rise above his station in life and the simple trappings of the poor jungle village he lived in. It was through his journey to death that Festus, perhaps for the first time in his life, was in control of his own destiny and could see his way forward clearly. He died a rich man.

He wears a Filipino Barong, a shirt made out of natural fibers that lets air move through it. It is the national dress shirt for men in the Philippines and, while it feels cool, Westerners always appear awkward wearing them—too tall in the saddle to look normal.

Ramsey keeps no council. He has no friends in the conventional sense, only acquaintances and colleagues. Even the Vietnamese, whose plight has occupied his adult life, do not enter his realm. In many respects it's as if he does not exist, although his office is the juncture between Asia and the United States for thousands of migrants. As Refugee Coordinator, he is the liaison for the Department of State, for INS, the U.S. Embassy and official U.S. government refugee programs.

More than a few backdoor operations move through his circle of knowledge—MIA/POW people, Army Intelligence, people who live and work in that nether world between official and unofficial duties—like Pete, who drank double scotches with me the night my son was born in Manila and who lives part of the year in Hanoi.

Most days at this time, Ramsey enters the Guest House to sit down at the lone piano. Before he begins to play he rests his hands on the keys and closes his eyes and quietly contemplates what is to come, recalling in his own mind the essence of the piece, its highs and lows, where it rises into lofty crescendos and where it falls down into the lowly depths where the agonies and mysteries of life perform.

He begins a search through his mind of the sights and sounds, even the smells and sweat-stained terror that is to come. This requiem bears little resemblance to Vivaldi or Mozart. Ramsey's god is more Wagnerian in its darkness, this an aria to the demons that haunt the dark side of humanity.

Ramsey memorized his requiem note by note over a seven-year period of torturous malarial captivity along the Cambodian frontier in the hands of the National Liberation Front—a military arm of the North Vietnamese. A disciple of John Paul Vann, he and Daniel Ellsberg were some of the first converts to Vann's methods of winning the hearts and minds of the Vietnamese people. Pretty heady company: Vann, one the most celebrated strategists of the Vietnam War and the principle character in one of the definitive books about the Vietnam conflict—Neil Sheehan's *Bright Shining Lie*; and Ellsberg, the man who released the "Pentagon Papers" and helped bring down a president.

Ramsey plays for a half hour, maybe forty-five minutes. His body moves to the madness of the music, his torso seeming to rise out of the piano bench. His eyes are closed, his hair blowing in the wind from the veranda, the muscles of his jaw and cheeks taut.

There is no musical score to guide his skillful playing. All of the music comes from his memory just as it did when he was creating it, building it note by note as a distraction, as a hypnotic balm, from his misery, all seven years and some odd days of his imprisonment. Each day he would replay in his mind what he had created the day before and the day before that until he could recall from memory, on an October day in another time and another place, every excruciating note.

If you listen closely, you can hear the ever-present fever that comes with malaria, hunger, dysentery, fear and pain. And if you close your eyes, you too can see the impenetrable jungle cage where he was kept, and you can hear the morning dew drip-drip-dripping as steam rises with each wakening breath, and you can watch each and every day die when hope descends in the shadows of the mountains.

Steve Toth

Life's Work

The local news man
 taunted me & he smiled
 Asked how does it feel
 knowing you've spent so much
 time & effort on something
 nobody cares about?

Is knowing better than not knowing?
 Who's the stranger here?
 It's true for the most part
 that poetry is uncalled for
 & you can't tell people
 what they should be reading

I paid no mind to the ones
 busy analyzing the personal
 into the sentimental
 Instead I listened
 to the ones who said stick
 to what you're good at

Some are afraid of the dark
 Others are afraid the darkness
 will leave them behind
 When will my life's work begin?
 Did language tell us apart?
 Is this a trick question?

Love Poem 19

I don't know what life is made of
but judging by
the amount of pain killers
we humans take
It must hurt like the dickins

Love is the good stuff
Love is what brings us together
Love is what connects us
Love has a life of its own
We didn't leave non-existence
to live in a world without love

You've got a way about you
I can't find my way without you
When the waves of pain come
roaring on the rocks
don't say "good-bye"
whisper "I love you"

Come On

First they lionize you
then they demonize you
Word gets around
Come on the writhing wind
with a pathological need
to be right
Caught in life's cross hairs
An earthquake will be
your only tsunami warning

That's the way they'll do you

The oil companies have
their pipes & the Native
Americans have theirs
I like a pipe organ with a beat
I can dance to along
with a few choice words
Oh but it's lonely at the top
of the food chain

Some people say "cheese"
when they take a picture
Others say "trees"
Just say what we're all thinking
I don't want my spirit crushed
What others call redundancy
I call incantation
Set your language on "stun"
I'm going to swallow my tears

Ashyer

James Petrillo

From the novel *Ashyer*—a Rocket Science Press new fantasy fiction release scheduled for Fall 2018

Frost heard the unmistakable sound of arrows leaving their strings and slicing through the air. Instinctively he leapt from the forest path. *Thunk thunk.* Two arrows pierced thick oak bark just inches from his head.

Twilight was giving way to blackness in the woods, but Frost used his heightened senses to investigate the black projectiles, quivering still, the shafts oily with a fetid residue reeking of goblins.

Strange, he thought, the wizard had never before summoned foul beasts during training. Perhaps this session was meant to be more difficult?

Just then, Frost felt knuckles against his neck as a hand grabbed his tunic from behind and pulled him into the undergrowth. At the same time a voice said, "Do you want to be a pin cushion?"

Frost spun to see Ty pointing across a field of tall grass at goblins armed with bows and knives.

"I count at least ten," Ty whispered.

Frost leaned close and whispered back, "What is Cirrus thinking sending goblins after us?"

Ty shrugged. "Maybe he's just stepping up the game."

"Something doesn't feel right. This does not feel like a game." Frost shook his head, then pointed. "Throw a decoy dart over there."

Throwing darts were Ty's weapon of choice. They were not as long as arrows and had short, feathered shafts and long, weighted, razor-sharp heads. Ty could throw one with some accuracy as far as sixty yards. Most were simple projectiles, but some were coated with colored potions and poisons. Some even glowed with magical enchantments.

Ty picked a simple dart and whipped it effortlessly into the undergrowth on the left side of the clearing. The goblins, hearing the rustle of thorn bushes where the dart had landed, stopped and turned to look. Frost and Ty watched the vile creatures grunting to each other in their guttural language. The creatures had mottled black-and-green skin, gnarled and wrinkled like a wart-wracked toad. They drooled from their sharpened teeth, and their eyes glowed in the dark like a cat's as they searched the spot where the dart had landed.

Quietly Frost gave his command. "I'll go straight in. You circle to the right."

Ty nodded and the two separated. The wind had picked up. Suddenly the air seemed charged with electricity. Frost noted the change immediately. "The wizard. Let's dispatch these wretches first. Then we'll deal with the wizard."

Frost reached under his cloak and quietly produced his unique bow. His own design, Frost had worked closely with both the bowyers and the weaponsmiths to produce a bow made entirely of steel. His was the most powerful and accurate bow in the kingdom, perhaps in the entire known world. A clever system of cables and pulleys allowed a steel bowstring to be used—an engineering marvel that had convinced some of his subjects that Frost might himself be a wizard.

He pulled three arrows from the quiver that hung from his belt. He saw Ty almost in position when the goblins turned back in his direction, their pig-like snouts twitching. *How can they smell anything but themselves*, he wondered, *putrid as they are?* He lightly planted two of the arrows in the soft ground at his feet and nocked the third to his string. Then he stood and revealed himself.

Upon spotting their quarry, the goblins triumphantly shrieked their earsplitting battle cry, but Frost was quicker than they supposed. Before they could begin their charge, the lead goblin was gazing wide-eyed at an arrow that had sprouted from the center of his chest. Before he had time to fall, two more were stung -- one with a killing shot to the neck; the other in its knobby thigh, the arrow passing through flesh and sinew out the other side.

Two were down and a third was limping, but that still left eight goblins now scampering over their fallen brethren and rushing on him with their knives drawn. Frost well knew that once they fell upon him it would render his death-raining weapon impotent.

But even as Frost continued to fire arrow after arrow on the advancing horde, a new volley began to whistle in from their left flank. Ty's darts found their marks with meaty thunks.

"Reap!" Ty yelled, a code word meant to signal Frost to close his eyes momentarily. The next dart he threw released its enchantment when it hit its target, sending out a spray of colorful but blinding sparks, similar to the magic fireworks they saw at the harvest celebration. The goblins hesitated in their charge, momentarily stunned and blinded.

"By the gods!" Ty yelled as he let fly yet another dart, "These buggers smell even worse when you fill them with holes and air them out!"

Frost cracked a smile, but his momentary amusement turned to panic when he opened his eyes post-fireworks display to see the shadowy silhouettes of several more goblins emerging from the trees *behind* Ty. Just as he was yelling a warning to his friend, an unusually large goblin -- barrel-chested, nearly as tall as a man, and draped in rough hide armor—picked up Ty and tossed him through the air.

Ty, with reflexes that would put a fox to the test, swung his arm back even as he was being thrown like a rag-doll, slicing the goblin's hand with the dart that he was about to throw. Then he was sailing twenty feet through the air, further into the center of the grassy clearing. Like a seasoned acrobat he rolled and was undamaged from the fall. He sprung to his feet again to fling the dart he still clutched at the beast that had just tossed him.

Unfortunately, the goblin's moldy hide armor turned aside the dart. It was not one of Ty's more graceful throws, heaving his projectile a goodly ways but lacking deadly force.

Fortunately, the enraged goblin suddenly became wobbly. Poison from the cut to his hand as he threw Ty was quickly taking effect. He staggered, taking a few more steps forward, grunted, and fell face-first to the ground. Only a ragged snore indicated he was still alive.

The others now hesitated. The remaining few backed off, as did the ones that had come in behind Ty. They regrouped around the edges of the clearing, taking stock.

"Leave me," Ty said to Frost with utter sincerity. "There are more coming in. We're outnumbered ten to one. I can hold them off while you make your escape, my Liege."

"Oh, don't get all formal on me now, for the first time in your life," Frost chided him. "I would never leave you, my friend."

Suddenly, lightning flashed above them, illuminating the hungry, greedy faces of the beasts all around. Frost shuddered at the sight of those faces, thinking, *They plan on eating us raw tonight.*

But the goblins' hateful faces began to register fear as the energy permeating the atmosphere intensified.

The wizard descended in an electromagnetic sphere.

Frost yelled, "Summoning goblins is a pretty dirty trick, Cirrus!"

"I suppose you had your eye on us the whole time?" Ty said. "Just waiting until the last moment to intervene?"

"I would never summon such vile filth!" The wizard boomed from above them.

Then, his voice came again, but this time as a whisper in their ears, a voice only they could hear. "This horde is not part of your exercise. Things are afoot that are well beyond my control."

Frost felt momentary vindication that his initial gut instinct had been right: Cirrus would never have done something like this, but the feeling was quickly replaced by a sinking feeling. *We're surrounded by goblins in a situation that is beyond the wizard's control?*

"What do we do, Cirrus?" Frost muttered under his breath, knowing the wizard would hear him.

Cirrus's answer was not terribly reassuring. "The goblins are held at bay by fear at the moment, but their hunger will soon prod them to a desperate, bestial bravery. I cannot kill them all. If I strike, the remaining ones will likely rip you two to pieces."

"We know all that," Ty said impatiently, "But do you have a plan?"

"Of course I do." The wizard's reply was tinged with mild annoyance. "When have you known me not to have a plan? When I strike them, Ty, throw your vial of fire potion straight up. Aim it at me. Put a good spin to it. Then, just before it hits me, Frost, fire an arrow directly at the center of its base. You must both be precise."

Ty shook his head as he produced the vial. "Sounds like a dicey plan."

"I didn't say it would work," Cirrus said. "Only that it is a plan."

Frost nocked an arrow. The goblins, seeing this action on the part of their prey, rallied, breaking the stalemate, and they rushed in.

"Now!" Cirrus's voice boomed.

Lightning crackled out from the wizard's sphere and roasted half the goblins. At the same moment Ty tossed the potion up, putting a fast spin on it. Frost, honed by hours of practice shooting thrown targets, took split-second aim and let loose the arrow. The bottle exploded. Due to the spin, its contents flew outward, raining down in a fiery ring around them. The grass all about the remaining goblins was set ablaze. Their ragged clothes and greasy hair catching fire, most of the inhuman creatures scattered and fled into the forest.

"We provided them the fire but denied them their supper to cook over it," Ty said. His nonchalant sense of humor never seemed to ebb, even in the midst of a life-or-death situation.

The sphere encasing the wizard settled to the ground, then it flickered like a candle flame and vanished. Cirrus stepped over a smoldering body and raised his staff. "Don't underestimate the tenacity of the hungry goblin. They have not all fled."

Ty produced a dagger. Down to his last two arrows, Frost readied his bow. True to Cirrus's pronouncement, several half-dead and even burning goblins rushed forward, their rage and hunger driving them to attack even in their death throes. The three men cut down the remaining predators until the only movement in the clearing was wisps of smoke from the smoldering grass.

After a few minutes of rest, the two young men stamped out the last burning patches, lest the whole forest go up. Cirrus even cast a spell that produced a shower of water on a tree that had begun to blaze. With that taken care of, the three set about the task of retrieving arrows and darts before they made their way into the woods. The battle might have drawn more unwanted attention, and they'd had their fill of goblins.

As they walked, just to break the silence, Ty said, "Well, old man, next time we do that exercise could you cut the numbers of the goblin horde down by about half?"

"I told you I had nothing to do with that—" Cirrus began to protest, but Frost intervened.

"Cirrus, you know he is just trying to get your goat."

"Well," the wizard grumbled, "I do not have a goat, and if I did I certainly would not give it to him. He would probably just try to steal it anyway." Cirrus frowned and looked severe, but both students could recognize the ever-so-slight flicker of amusement in Cirrus's voice. If it had been lighter out, they knew they'd see that tale-tell quiver at the corner of his mouth, indicating he was suppressing a chuckle.

Though a magician of some repute, Cirrus was actually not quite old enough to be their father. He felt like an older brother, or an uncle, perhaps. Although he tried to be firm and harsh with them, the wizard was fond of both boys. *Young men, now,* he thought. *Soon to be called upon to take on their responsibilities as men. Sooner, perhaps, than we thought. Xan, my King, I hope we have prepared them well.*

After that brief exchange, they fell into silence, as if the weight of the night was now settling in on them, and they turned inward to their own melancholy thoughts.

Frost's wavy, dark brown hair fell wildly down his back. He thought, *What would the ladies of the court think if they saw their prince in such a state*, and smiled. His tunic and cloak were black, since the training exercise was supposed to have been one in forest stealth. At nineteen, he was still sheltered from most of the pressures and responsibilities of state, and he generally had a carefree air of happiness about him. Ty probably had something to do with that: ever since he had come to live with Frost in the palace, that insubordinate thief from the streets was dependable for deflating any tendency toward pomposity or showy formality.

Ty followed close behind him, always alert even if his casual bearing did not show it. Ty, the same age as Frost, was shorter and slighter, but he was quite agile. His blonde hair was tied back tight so it would make no noise, and any but the most sensitive forest tracker listening to their footfalls would swear there were only two men passing through the woods.

The wizard led the way, a soft glow at the tip of his staff acting as a lantern. Though his dark hair was beginning to show streaks of gray and he had a slightly sallow look, he had only seen seventeen summers more than his pupils. He wore a dark blue robe that seemed to be sewn from the fabric of twilight itself. He led them carefully up a hill toward the Great Road.

The moon had started to rise as they cleared the forest, and they all stopped to look at it for a moment. As always, they were struck with wonder at its beauty coupled with dread at what it had brought to their world, the world of Ashyer.

The "moon" of Ashyer was, in fact, a planet. Its orbit had brought it ever closer the past few weeks. The time was drawing near when it would pass its closest to Ashyer. As it rose, the moon filled half the horizon with its sickly yellow light. Later that night it would fill most of the sky, and they would be able to make out some surface features of that terrible world.

Once every year it happened, what some of Ashyer's inhabitants called—generally under their breath and with accompanying warding hand gestures—the "Murder Moon." It meant one thing for all the peoples of Ashyer: The dragons would come to pillage all the settlements, from the lowliest hamlet to the greatest kingdom. The only protection from utter destruction was to broker a deal with the dragons.

Cirrus shook his head at the moon dismissively and continued walking. Pushing away their own thoughts of the coming dragons, Ty and Frost followed.

"There are always a few living here on Ashyer," Cirrus said as they resumed their hike. "Dragons I mean. Some of them stay behind. I was just thinking about them."

Frost cast another involuntary glance at the yellow blight on the horizon. "How can you not, with that thing in the sky to remind us?"

"'Twas not always so, Fredris. Since your father is one of the last of the immortals, he can remember a time when that cursed moon did not appear in the sky."

"Can't you just call me Frost?" Frost replied with more irritation in his voice than he'd intended. "You did when we were in battle."

"Very well, Prince Frost, as you command."

Ty started to chuckle.

"*Prince* Frost? That's even worse." Frost said, deliberately modulating his voice back to a more casual register.

"Like it or not, Frost, you may be king someday. Whether your father be immortal or not." Cirrus's statement sounded rather enigmatic, but before Frost could prod him and try to unravel this riddle, Cirrus crested the hill.

Frost caught up and looked down. On the other side of the hill only a few miles east lay the ocean and the capitol city of Olan; the castle, his home, on the top of a hill southeast of the port and south of Olan Bay. "Father *is* an immortal, so I don't think I have to worry about that."

Ty joined them, sounding much more serious than usual when he said, "There's a reason he is one of the last, Frost."

Cirrus glanced at Ty, then turned back to Frost. "I would not have put it quite that way, but Master Ty is right. Your father is an immortal, but he is not indestructible."

Frost frowned in thought. "We have had peace in Olan for centuries, though, since we made the deal with the dragons."

Cirrus looked to the south. "Things change, Frost," he said quietly.

Frost turned to follow Cirrus's gaze. Only a half mile off, the Great Road crested a hill. The road had existed since before Olan and was therefore a mystery. Two parallel stone corridors, the Great Road was wide enough to put three wagons across on either side. It stretched from one ocean to the other on its westward journey. Usually only a few caravans or adventurers traveled it, but on that night, it seemed the entire army of Olan streamed westward upon its ancient stones. From their vantage point on the hill, the three of them could see the column of men marching toward a camp just to the southwest of their position. The sound of horses and armor reached their ears.

"Who are we fighting?" Ty asked.

"King Xan Olan received a message of a massive goblin army approaching from the west only days ago. His scout confirmed it just this day. I did not expect any to have come far enough east yet for us to encounter them in your training."

"What do they think they are doing?" Frost said, perhaps a tad boastfully. "We will wipe them clean of this land without losing a single man."

"The goblins are allied with the dragons," Cirrus said. "We do not yet know what this may mean."

"We will join them," Frost declared boldly and began toward the camp.

Cirrus grabbed his arm. "I've given my word to your father that I would keep you away. I am sorry."

Frost eyed the wizard suspiciously. "I suppose that means you would use magic if necessary?"

With no malice, Cirrus said, "Yes. I *am* sorry. However, we can camp near the road and build a fire, so we may see what is to come, if you wish."

"I suppose that's the best I can get, huh?" As if weighing the prospects and suddenly making peace with the situation, Frost shrugged, smiling, and said, "Come on, Ty, let's go make camp."

The three walked along the hilltop south toward the Great Road, collecting scraps of wood as they went. When they were close enough to be identified by the passing army as allies, they stopped and built a small fire. Cirrus produced a wine skin and some salted meat and passed it to Frost. Ty tended to the fire and then joined his companions, sitting down cross-legged in the grass.

"There in the distance, Frost, can your remarkable eyes see it?" Cirrus was pointing.

"Fires. Maybe hundreds."

Ty strained to make out anything and shook his head resignedly. "I don't see a thing. I wish I had your bloodline, Frost. Or at least your *eye*-line."

"You can have it. Besides, you have long-blood in you. Your mother was long-born."

Ty shook his head again. "It doesn't make me long nor does it let me see any better."

Cirrus looked appraisingly at the two. "No one can predict the outcome of the mingling of the blood. Many have remarked upon your uncanny dexterity, Ty. As if your mother had been a cat."

Ty lifted an eyebrow. "A cat, eh? You know, I *could* take that the wrong way."

Frost, seeing an opportunity perhaps to pry some information from their normally private and tight-lipped teacher, chimed in. "So, I guess I've never asked … how did you end up with wizard's blood?"

"Well, let me think." The wizard produced a smoking pipe from a pocket in his robe, tamped in some tobacco from another pocket, and lit the pipe with a twig from the fire.

Ty rolled his eyes. "Great. Here comes a history lesson."

Frost punched him in the shoulder. "I want to know; shut it." Ty rubbed his shoulder and grinned. Frost didn't pull his punches much, but the gesture between the two of them was always friendly. Only once had they ever struck each other in anger, and that was before they knew they were destined to become Bloodtwins, sword brothers, companions of the heart.

Cirrus cleared his throat. "As you should know well by now—or would if you were as eager for your book studies as you are for dashing about brandishing your weapons for the ladies in the practice yard—the world of Ashyer was originally inhabited by three races: Angels, Immortals, and Giants. The sky, the land, and below. It was the mingling of the blood that made the rest of us. Angels and Immortals created the long men who have the power of magic hidden in their blood, though most cannot tap it. Immortals and Giants created the common men, who have no magic as far as anyone knows. And, in some terrible acts of cruelty, Angels and Giants created demons and all the foul spawn that wander the wilds, like those goblins marching from the west. Wizards came from the mingling of long and common blood, for it seems that in some common men and women lies the key to unlocking the magic of the long blood. Sometimes it takes generations for the key to surface. For me it was two generations ago. My grandfather was of common blood. To my knowledge, that is how my father and I gained the ability to cast and to speak to the elements."

They all looked at the fire for a time, then Ty spoke up. "Has anyone ever seen an angel, the sky women?"

Cirrus shook his head. "Not in living memory has anyone seen an angel. Unfortunately, the race of winged women was decimated when the dragons arrived."

Frost, still staring intently into the fire, asked, "Is my father the last one, the last Immortal?"

"I don't know, Frost." After a short silence, during which he took a long, thoughtful draw from his pipe, Cirrus added, "Your father is a good man, but not all Immortals were. Just as not all Giants were either giant or evil, not all Immortals were noble or honorable. Some of them were the worst tyrants this world has ever known. Sometimes … Sometimes I hope he *is* the last."

"You missed a race," Ty said. "The offspring of Angels and Demons."

"I would not call those disgusting affronts to nature a race, but yes. The undead were the spawn of a tortured angel at the hands of a demon. A mix of magic and the dead, horror beyond horror."

Frost was in his own thoughts and not following the conversation. Speaking his own thoughts aloud again, he asked, "How long do you think I will live?"

Cirrus raised an eyebrow. "How long do you think I will?"

Frost caught the wizard's meaning and chuckled, "Point taken."

The fire crackled and started to die out. The fully risen moon provided ample light to see the progress of the army, however, and the three companions watched the slow progression.

Cirrus knocked the ashes of his pipe into the remains of the fire, rolled onto his side and said, "Get some rest, boys."

Ty slapped his knee. "We're *men*, old man."

Cirrus smiled. "As you will, Master Ty."

Ty and Frost continued to watch the dying embers as they winked out, one by one.

Speaking more quietly so as not to wake the wizard, Ty asked, "Do you remember the day we met?"

"You mean the day you stalked me to rob me?"

"I wasn't actually going to rob you. Someone needed to watch your back. What kind of prince wanders out to a forest lake alone to go swimming?"

Frost lay down on his side and muttered, "You had no idea who I was until you went through my things."

"I was just curious. I wanted to know what kind of things a prince might take swimming."

"Sure." Frost's eyes closed. He said something else, but it was an incoherent mumble that trailed away, weary exhaustion finally overtaking him.

Ty grinned. "Nothing very valuable unfortunately," he said to no one in particular. He lay down beside his companions on the soft grass in the sickly moonlight. For a while he stared up at the moon. He could see tiny red mountain ranges, as if he were floating above looking down on them. He wondered what Ashyer looked like from over there, and then he was asleep.

Cirrus was shaking them. Frost and Ty opened their eyes to see the wizard crouched between them. The moon had not travelled far in the time they had slept. Only a couple of hours had passed. Frost looked to the road, but no soldiers were there. There was a great rumbling noise coming from the west. He sat up quick, and Cirrus held his shoulder tight.

From their vantage point the three could see, perhaps only a mile off, the army of Olan assembled at the base of the hill before a horde of thousands of goblins.

The goblins were banging swords and growling, their inhuman voices carrying up to their perch atop the hill. The knights were organizing ranks with shield bearers in the front to protect the archers. The goblins stood like a mob, pushing and yelling. Frost thought they looked like a filthy ocean that was threatening to spill over the army. That was when he realized the gravity of the situation. The goblins could win. Their numbers were enormous. Had his father wanted him out of the city in case they lost? Then he spotted it: his father's pavilion.

"He's down there!" Frost yelled at Cirrus.

"I know, Frost. Please stay here," Cirrus said calmly.

A tear threatened to spill from Frost's eye, and he wiped at it. "We could lose. He could be killed."

"Your father is not so easily beaten, Frost."

Before any more could be said, trumpets sounded and the army loosed arrows on the horde. Hundreds of goblins died in the first volley, but the rest seemed unswayed. A wave of thousands of goblins surged toward the army. More arrows flew, and the front line of goblins fell again, but it was not enough. Swords were unsheathed, and man met goblin in combat. As the two forces clashed, the sound was deafening.

"Look!" Ty was pointing to the forest to the south.

The others saw what Ty had spotted. The mounted knights of Olan rode out from cover at full charge on their armored horses. Each horse was outfitted with razor sharp spikes. The Knights crashed into the ocean of goblins at full charge without slowing. They left a mangled trail of broken bodies in their wake.

The mob was thinning, and the goblins looked as if they were starting to scatter when there was a terrible *crack* from the sky. All looked up and saw it. An enormous dragon was streaking down to the battle.

Frost tried to leap to his feet, but Cirrus forced both him and Ty to lie down in the grass. They raised their heads only enough to see. The dragon was flying low over the battlefield as if assessing the state of affairs. Then, apparently deciding it was a lost cause for the goblins, it started breathing fire on everything, man and goblin alike.

Frost tried to wiggle free, but Cirrus held fast. The dragon circled around and inhaled deep. It was lining up behind the fleeing Knights of Olan. Just as the Knights reached the forest line, it exhaled massive flame, destroying trees and Knights as one. Frost dropped his face into the grass and began to weep. It was the voice of his father that made him raise his head again.

"Hear me, dragon!" Xan Olan stood on a small hill at the edge of the battle. His voice was barely audible over the chaos and fire. "Face me!"

The dragon turned in flight and landed in front of Xan. The battlefield was a scorched waste with very little moving.

"You have violated our agreement," the voice of the dragon boomed.

Then Xan was talking, but his voice could not be heard from the hill where the three lay in hiding.

"Spare me your lies," the dragon answered whatever Xan had said. "You have created a forbidden weapon and will be destroyed!"

Before Frost could wonder what that meant, they heard another *crack* behind them. The three looked around and saw another dragon diving toward the castle.

"No—" Frost began, but before he could utter any kind of pointless plea, the dragon enveloped the castle in relentless fire. Frost was about to scream, but it was the scream of his father he heard. The three turned to look at the battlefield once more. The dragon that had accused his father was breathing fire in a steady stream. The figure of Xan Olan was silhouetted for a moment, then engulfed, and finally turned to ash.

Frost leaped to his feet. His blood quickened; the wizard too slow to stop him. Pulling his bow, the archer ran at a non-human pace toward the dragon.

The appearance of Frost caught the dragon off guard. Frost did not hesitate. He released two steel arrows almost simultaneously and struck the dragon in both eyes, piercing the soft ocular flesh easily. Fire exploded from the wounded sockets almost instantly, shooting straight at Frost, but Cirrus and Ty arrived in time to deflected the flames and pull Frost to the ground.

"Quiet, you fool," Cirrus hissed into Frost's ear.

The dragon roared and spit flame wildly. Tents and pavilions were engulfed all around them. Finally, the dragon took off. Roaring in pain and smoking from the eyes, it flew toward the moon. The three watched as it was joined by the other dragon and disappeared into the yellow sky.

Frost buried his face in the scorched grass and wept. Cirrus and Ty continued to stare dumbstruck at the moon. When they were sure there were no more dragons coming, Ty and Cirrus sat up. Frost clenched his head with his hands and wept harder. Ty started to reach for his friend, but Cirrus stayed him. "Let him be for a moment, Master Ty."

Cirrus and Ty rose and walked toward the battlefield so as to give Frost some space, barely taking their eyes off the moon.

"Do they really fly to the moon?" Ty asked in a low quivering voice. "That seems impossible."

"It does seem impossible," Cirrus answered. "I am not an expert on the heavens, but such a feat must be assisted with powerful magic, I would suppose."

"I thought dragons couldn't use magic. That's why they raid Ashyer." Tears wet Ty's cheeks as he looked at the carnage before them.

"It is a mystery, Master Ty. How it is done, I cannot guess. But perhaps it is not the dragon's own magic, but a magic stolen from an older time that allows them to accomplish the feat." Cirrus' eyes fell upon someone he recognized lying dead, and he squeezed them tight to avert tears.

Frost had risen and was walking toward his father's ashes. Cirrus and Ty watched but made no attempt to interfere. Reaching the smoking mound, Frost knelt before it. He bowed his head and sat back on his heels and wept. Ty and Cirrus turned away, giving privacy to his grief.

"I hardly knew him. King Xan." Ty said quietly to Cirrus, "I was practically raised as Frost's brother, but the king was always away."

"I knew him well," Cirrus said flatly. "He sent me to the wizard school in the south, and I became his most trusted advisor."

After a moment of contemplation and more tears, Ty said, "So it's true then. Dragons explode when they are killed. We saw fire stream out of its pierced eyes."

"Indeed, it is true. Had Frost shot for the heart and found a space between scales, none of us would be standing here. In fact, this battlefield would have been completely wiped clean by the blast. But, I think Frost knew that. He wanted to mark the dragon that killed his father, not destroy himself and us."

The sound of rustling from behind them made Ty and Cirrus turn around. Frost was sliding his hands into the ashes. Ty cringed, but Cirrus quickly started walking toward Frost.

"Frost—" Cirrus began.

Before Cirrus could finish, Frost had pulled a longsword of incredible quality from the ashes. Its blade was almost twice the length of a normal longsword and had a blue steel look about it. More than that, the blade's edges twinkled as if sprinkled with diamonds. As Frost turned it in his hands it glowed slightly with powerful magic. The weapon should have weighed as much as a two-handed sword, but it felt light as a feather in Frost's hands. He reached to touch the blade.

"Stop!" Cirrus yelled. "One touch could kill you!"

Frost did not touch the blade, but he fixed Cirrus with an accusing stare. "The dragon said a forbidden weapon had been made. How much do you know? You tell me wizard!"

Cirrus put his hand up in surrender. "I will tell you all, my king, but not here. We need to hide that sword."

At the words "my king," Frost dropped the sword. Ty, always with an eye for value, grabbed a fallen Olan banner and ran to it. He delicately rolled the beautiful weapon tightly in the cloth and tried to hand it back to Frost. His eyes on the battlefield now, Frost did not seem to notice the gesture and started walking toward the dead. Ty then turned and tried to offer the sword to Cirrus.

"You carry it for him for now, Master Ty. There will come a time that he will take it up on his own. Until then, remain his true friend and keep it safe. It is very important."

As he tied it under his cloak on his back, Ty asked, "What is it?"

Cirrus kept his eyes on Frost and clenched his teeth. "A sword, Master Ty, a sword that could alter the destiny of Ashyer."

Hours passed and Frost was returning to his companions on the hill, where they had gathered wood and relit their fire from the night before. In his hands Frost carried a few small items.

When he reached them he held out his hand to Ty. In his palm was the symbol of the Captain of the Royal Guard, a small white shield pendant with two down-pointing crossed green swords. Ty accepted it without a word. Frost then held his other hand to Cirrus. For him, Frost had found a dagger of the Order of Knights. Cirrus also accepted without a word. The last item was a scrap of purple fabric. Only one person was wearing purple cloth on the battlefield, Xan Olan. Frost tied his hair in the back using the scrap.

"So we shall not forget the sacrifices of this day," Frost said in a somber tone. It was a tone neither Cirrus nor Ty had ever heard from him before. He seemed about ten years older. He sat by the fire and looked at Cirrus. "Now my teacher, teach me. What has transpired this day?"

Cirrus rubbed at his forehead for a moment, collecting his thoughts before he began.

"Your father knew the peace with the dragons could not last. He saw how greedy the dragon-kind are and knew they would continue to demand more each year, which they have. Also, he saw the toil of the people to keep up with the demand. He did not want the people of Olan to suffer their entire lives with no end to it. So, he began his plan. Other kingdoms have gone to war with the dragons, but all have fallen because, as you know, if you kill a dragon, the furnace within explodes destroying everything.

"He needed to create something that could battle a dragon and survive the encounter. He found the best sword-smiths and enchanters in the land, and in secret bid them make such a weapon. This year he was presented with the sword that master Ty has on his back. The blade is eternally sharp and can pierce even stone, but that's not the incredible part. The reason I told you not to touch the blade is because of the enchantment it holds. Whatever it strikes is frozen solid. This a dragonslayer blade, the only of its kind ever imagined, one that can pierce the heart of a dragon, extinguishing its fire along with its life."

Cirrus paused to gaze out at the battlefield. "This was not part of the plan. The dragons must have had spies that warned them of the impending attack and decided to strike first. While the goblin army distracted Olan, the other dragon destroyed the castle. It was that action that made King Xan hesitate I think, for otherwise he would have slain the dragon with the sword. It was in that second that the dragon killed your father. You, Frost, are what the dragon did not count on. I'm sure it would have gathered up the sword and destroyed it had you not attacked at that very moment. But now we have the Dragon Slayer, the Fire Douser. And perhaps we can start to change the destiny of our world."

Frost looked into the fire for a long moment before speaking. "You let me go. You didn't actually try to stop me from attacking the dragon because you knew what was at stake." His gaze shifted from the fire to Cirrus.

Cirrus looked away. "Yes, my king, I knew if the dragon destroyed the blade, we were all as good as dead anyway."

Silence fell, broken only by the cawing of distant crows and vultures gathering on the field, and the crackling of the small fire.

Ty was the first to break the silence. "Well, at least you're a good shot, Frost. Saving the world … that could take some time."

Frost did not respond to this, but when he spoke a moment later it was with a sorrow heavier than any of them had ever known. "My mother was in the castle."

Ty found tears rising into his own eyes, and he buried his face in his cloak.

Cirrus lowered his head and nodded.

Frost lay himself down and closed his eyes. Ty reached to comfort him, putting his hand on his friend's shoulder, and Cirrus did not stop him.

"Rest, men, for there are dark times ahead. I fear we will be on the run from dangers we can scarcely imagine now." He pulled out his pipe and his tobacco pouch, because, for the moment, there was nothing else to be done.

Three Poems
Steve Schild

Excerpt from the collection *These Humans,* an Up On Big Rock new release scheduled for Fall 2018

Nightly News

For John Berryman, Henry, the eminent Dr. Bones

"A satellite circled striated Jupiter
from a quarter-million miles away
and sent back photos
technicians will splice together
to study the planet's composition.
It is speculated that Earth's atmosphere
was similar in its early stages,
but we know virtually nothing
about this largest planet,
only that it has thirteen moons
and, just south of its equator, a mysterious
red blotch three times the circumference of Earth.

"Closer to home,
a Portage farmer, a 'quiet family man
with no financial problems and an
outstanding work record,'
shotgunned his wife and sons
last night, then turned the gun on himself.
He had been despondent lately, 'sick to death
of winter. All we can figure out,' intoned the coroner,
'is that the weather was getting him down.'

"Also yesterday, authorities made official
the death of young Chester Metcalfe, who
'clung precariously to life,' battled irreversible
brain damage more than two days after being discovered
frozen in a snowbank. There was no visible
evidence of a struggle or injury."

All of these investigators and scientists puzzled

while the four of us sprawl here drunk
even before the bourbon, half-buzzed
by the nightly news but seeing clearly as any
that on this inauspicious day it rained,
first rain of Spring (so it is called, but
Someone may be teasing; we weren't
convinced because the rain kept on freezing).
Should we tell them, boys, should we give them
a measure on the world and the weather?
—No; it's like the price of a yacht,
a luxury, this knowing—if you gotta ask . . .
Let's have another drink;
let's sigh and be certain
there is only this season,
have a laugh while they try
to coax us sober with Reason.

Three Ways

I.
Go on as if nothing happened.
Shave. Tie your tie.
Kiss your pretty wife,
whether awake or asleep
or in dream or real life,
goodbye. Remember
that your routine
remains the same;
those you know and love
will still be themselves,
clocks will run the same circle,
numbers yield the same sum,
yet something is different beyond description
and shall never
not be so.

II.
Hide as long as you can.
Come out only in dire need
or absent any chance of escape.
When asked anything,
deny everything;
say that you never saw, never knew,
never thought through why you should
do anything but
follow along, sing the same song
as those all around you,
glass-eyed and safe.

III.
Do what you can.
Read the age spots on your skin
like a watch, knowing no timepiece
is perfect. Sleep deep; resist
only when it offers some sort of
chance, and know that winning may change
nothing of substance, and that it may
kill you, too. Make your peace
with books lost or long overdue,
with those left on the shelf
you never got to.
Look for a sign in the turn
of each leaf; make sense of the world
as you would a lover's fitful sleep.

Tibetan Monks Visit Terrace Heights

There are piles of work to do,
but you sit talking
to an old man, killing time,
letting it run through your hands
like sand.

Nearby, someone's child
is about to die of a broken heart
or some other dark dead end
in the warren of woe and want
that is the world we inhabit;
but because it is beyond your reach
you shuffle papers, you run in place as if
you could escape from or file away or seal or heal
the break that is the hole in the world's heart.

And then, as you try to hide from or ignore
such phantoms that haunt and taunt you,
that forever elude, that refuse to
stop and fight or fly away,
the visiting monks, just back from lunch,
appear in blood-colored robes of Zen
and look past you and all you feel so bad about;
wielding metal tools,
they work like worms with infinitesimal grains of sand
and colors to make a picture of the world
that always has at its heart
the mantra that when this gorgeous thing is finished
the wind will sneeze and take it away,
and with it tomorrows and yesterdays,
leaving what is left for only you to say.

Nowhere to go & Old Gus speaks
Dan Coffey

Photo by Dan Coffey

Nowhere to go and nothing to do

We didn't notice any explosions. Our first clue was when the Internet went down. A few minutes later we noticed no cell phone service.

There was no reason to panic, it might have been a storm. When we checked the TV, some stations were still on the air. They were playing movies and game shows. But no news.

They say that people ninety miles from the big cities could hear the booms. People in Rockford, Illinois could hear the bombs in Chicago. They were deep, prolonged booms, but not terribly loud at that distance. Those who had been looking in that direction saw flashes, but not everybody was looking that way. Most people were indoors.

It turns out that it wasn't a big attack, like the one we had all learned to expect from Russia. Only four cities were targeted. LA, New York, Chicago and Washington. Only a few bombs per city. No one knew who was behind it, or whether President Trump was still alive. Many people hoped he wasn't.

It took a week before regular radio and television broadcasting resumed. Light entertainment predominated. News was a somber affair. White men wearing jacket and tie intoned facts and figures like funeral directors. There was still no report on the status of the President, nor most members of government. By now, cellphone service had resumed in many places, but not all. The Internet was still down.

At night, bands of orange flickered overhead like the northern lights. There was a smell like burning wires. It became very hot for about a week, then smoke filled the sky and the temperature plummeted. Even though it was mid-summer, we had to wear jackets during the day. The plants that had survived the hot spell, soon withered and died in the cold gloom. Farmers threw in the towel.

We who lived in rural America paid the price for having let our towns decline. Now there was no getting away to the city. Gas prices went up by a factor of twenty, and there were road blocks on most major highways, so there was nowhere to go and nothing to do in town.

Those towns big enough to have a Wal Mart didn't suffer much for the first month, but after that the shelves had been picked clean. Since everything Wal-Mart sells was made in China anyway, and because the prices of those items had doubled during the trade war, people were already used to getting by with less. Now they were going to have to get even more resourceful.

The hunger came on more quickly than anyone realized. After only six weeks, there were food shortages. After eight weeks, people were starting to die. At first it was the young, old, and infirm who succumbed, but after three months, mornings found bodies stacked during the night on almost every street corner.

Nobody was ever certain who had attacked us, or why. The theory most people accepted was that it had started with a nuclear exchange between India and Pakistan, and then somehow had spread to Israel, Iran, North Korea, and finally to us. Since no missiles had been fired at us, it was thought that the bombs had already been in place, on the ground, waiting to be detonated at a any date. But as to who put them there or pressed the trigger, no one knew for certain.

After a year, things started to get better. It turns out that almost no on in Washington survived. Leaders from other states were brought in. There was a lot of talk of retaliation, but nothing was ever done because we didn't know who to invade or bomb. You can't just bomb everyone. We've tried that in the past, and it doesn't work. Or maybe it gets you where we are today.

Old Gus Speaks

I was hoping somebody like you would come along. Been waiting a long time. Sit down. We've got some talking to do.

They say I have brain damage. They say that, at best, I've got two more years. What do they know? They might only have six months. Maybe six days. What do they know?

I once dated a girl who was in the Miss America contest. That was back in the fifties. She had a good figure and an even better face. In the "show how smart you are" part of the contest, I thought she stole the show. She talked about Eisenhower warning America to beware of the Military/Industrial Complex.

Nobody had the faintest idea what that girl was talking about. But they gave her polite applause when she was done. She might have won or placed if she'd just kept mum about Eisenhower.

Most of the girls talked about the role of proper nutrition and discipline at home to have a happy family. That's what people wanted to hear a young woman talk about back then.

As I recall, she later married a guy who owned some hotels in Kansas City and Des Moines. They had the money, so they traveled a lot. I remember hearing that they were killed in an automobile accident in Panama.

I've got a lot of stories. Most of them aren't uplifting. People generally don't want to hear many of them. Children avoid me. I've been told my face is etched in a permanent scowl.

But I'm not angry. No, as dispositions go, I'm sanguine. That's an old-fashioned word for mellow. I can take it or leave it, roll with the punches, have my cake and eat it too. I don't need to be well-liked.

Guy like me doesn't remember insults, so he can't form resentments. Water off a duck's back. Sure, every once in a while, I lose my cool, grab a gun or a knife and start stalking somebody or other, but most people can outrun me. Then I get thirsty or hungry or tired and can't remember what all the fuss was about.

The cops in this town know where I live. For a while the doctors had me on lithium, but that just gave me a headache and made me thirsty. Kept me out of trouble because I never felt good enough to leave the house.

Believe it or not, I hope to hook up with a woman again someday. A younger woman. Women my age don't do much for me. As I recall, they don't care much for me, either. Maybe one of those third-world women who will take any old geezer provided he can get them far away from where they came from. That's a service I could provide. She could service me in lots of ways.

Someday it will all be about pooping and peeing and remembering to take your meds. If you don't take them, it's a problem, if you take them twice, it's a bigger problem. That day hasn't arrived yet. Until it does, I'm gonna get away with as much as possible.

If I could suddenly get involved in something highly lucrative and slightly illegal, I would, but for the life of me, I don't have the faintest idea what that might be. You gotta know something about drugs to be a drug dealer. Any idiot can rob a bank, but the payout isn't big and the risk is astronomical.

I'd risk it all for a big enough payout. Something that would substantially change my life circumstances. Right now I've got an application in for the senior center in town. They give you a room and meals for whatever your social security check is. I visited a friend or two there over the years and the place always smells like pee. There's a big room with a TV and nobody's really watching it. Some old ladies slumped over in wheelchairs along the wall. Fat nurses talking too loud and trying too hard to be cheerful. That kind of place.

That's the kind of place that on a really cold winter night, I'd let myself out the side door and wander off into a snowdrift, just to put an end to it. If that's all I have to look forward to, why not just get it over with?

But if I had a few hundred thousand dollars of cash, I could probably run off to one of those banana republics and do all right.

You say you got to be somewhere else? All right then, been nice talking to you. Good luck young man. From what I've seen of this world, you're gonna need it.

Three Poems
Rob Hardy
Poet Laureate of Northfield, Minnesota

Jane Austen's House at Chawton
Written in Kenilworth, Warwickshire, U.K.

These Hampshire hills, so brown in winter,
and all this mud! How dull it must have been
for the girl with her mind on balls, the flirt
and dreamer with nothing to do indoors
but invent lovers and impossible odds,
or publish imaginary banns for herself
in copies of the parish register. But how ideal
for the sensible woman who sits and writes,
who has stopped imagining happiness
for herself, and so creates it for someone else—
this rain-blurred world refocused in her mind
into images so sharp they stand out
from everything here, all this furniture
borrowed from the written world.

Reading *Rebecca,* Far from Home

Du Maurier understood homesickness:
she filled a book with it,
with the remembered scent
of crushed azalea petals,
with the rhododendrons hemorrhaging into bloom,
the moan of wood pigeons haunting the woods
like voices speaking softly in another room.
She knew the slips and evasions of memory,
and how it can sometimes hurt to get too close
to something so distant.
Better to forget oneself in the strange,
indifferent sea.

Light
November 9, 2016

Through the sleepless night Orion
still strode above the rooftops of the town.
The sunrise still unfurled its pink and blue
as if announcing a birth. The sun still rose,
and as it rose it burnished the prairie grass.
Nothing had been taken from the beauty of the world.
Even the raucous geese were beautiful
with the light of morning on their wings.
Even the gray November woods were filled with light.
A young woman stepped from the path
to walk in the fallen leaves,
just for the pleasure of the music they made.
The leaves whispered at her feet.
The light seemed to rise up from the earth,
up the stems of the grass, into the bare branches of the trees.
The light was all around us. And still it rises.

Transport and the Zipper Lady

Nancy Palker

From the memoir *Tragic and Magic Rosebud,* a Lost Lake Folk Art new release scheduled for 2019.

Bravery. *Woohitike (wo-oh-hee-tee-keh).* Having or showing courage.

From a photo by Nance Palker

We called her the Zipper Lady. The nurse from St. Anthony's Flying Service reminded us of the *"Cherry Ames, Flight Nurse"* book we had read as young girls. In her 30s, with brown hair pulled back oh so neatly, she wore a blue jumpsuit with a zillion zippers for all her snazzy high-tech equipment and doodads. Larger than life, a superhero to us, she carried on efficiently as she prepared the sickest patients to be airlifted to a proper medical center in Rapid City, South Dakota, Lincoln, Nebraska, or sometimes Denver, Colorado. We Rosebud staff members would gather with our noses pressed against the nursery window, enthralled as she deftly whisked a baby off to the waiting plane. The only surprise was that it didn't happen more often, as we were pitifully understaffed, undertrained, and undersupplied. The Zipper Lady's appearance always seemed to save the day. We did our best with what we had, but like the rest of the reservation, our resources were meager at best.

As a newly budding nurse, I had decided that I would never do something to a patient that I hadn't experienced myself. Shortly after I had devised that great idea, I received a doctor's order to pass an NG tube, which was about 1/4" diameter going up one's nose, down the throat and into the stomach. I understood why that patient needed this procedure and I did not, and thus ended that naive resolution.

Another principle we'd learned in nursing school was to use "nursing measures" before giving sleep medication, if possible, to avoid unwanted side effects of the meds. Sometimes repositioning or adjusting the pillow could solve the problem, though we discovered that it worked more often in books than in practice. Often a combination of nursing and meds worked best. About ten o'clock one night, the man at the end of the hall asked for a sleeping pill. Following the nursing theory, I had learned in school, I first went to his room without the pill, and offered him a backrub to relax him, which was then standard practice on the evening shift. He gladly accepted the backrub, but moments after I started, I felt his hands rubbing MY backside, so I quickly got him his chloral hydrate pill to knock him out for the night, standing at an arm's length away to hand it to him with a glass of water. After that, he got all of his meds regularly from me, administered from a distance, minus the backrubs.

Mr. Arnold was our dear Assistant Director of Nurses, our mentor and champion. He took full advantage of any lull in the action to teach us about anything and everything. We had so much to learn! When we'd complain about feeling uncomfortable in a situation, he would say, "A nurse is a nurse and can function anywhere." We'd reply that we weren't really nurses yet, still waiting to hear whether or not we'd passed our nursing board exams. I clearly remember starting my first IV. I was mortified that the patient was an alert attractive young man, about my age. "Oh, why couldn't it be a sleepy old person?" I lamented. Mr. A. replied that he chose this guy because of his good veins, so it would be easier for me. Physically easier, probably, but the guy's mocking sassy attitude over my trepidation made me even more nervous. Fortunately for both of us, I did hit his vein on the first try and got the IV started.

Then there was the CVP, central venous pressure. For really sick patients, it's not enough to check their blood pressure in their arm, but there would be an IV line going into the main vein to the heart – all measurements that are automated in today's ICU. In that time, we had only a glass tube contraption almost two feet tall with teeny markings. We had to attach this tube to the central IV line, then rest the tube by the patient's chest, and try to line it up vertically by eyeballing it with the door frame to get it perpendicular for a supposedly accurate measurement. That was pretty much state of the art for the time.

After about two weeks on the job, I was given the medication room keys and assigned to pass meds for the 25 patients on the unit. We had a pharmacy, but medicines back then came in big stock bottles shared by all patients on the unit. We had little two- inch handwritten cards for each med for each patient, teeny ruffled paper cups in which to pour the pills, plastic cups for the liquid doses, and a tray with a slot for the cards by the hole for the cup. We had to triple check each patient's name, med, and dose as we poured the pills. It took me a couple of hours to painstakingly organize all these doses, with interruptions for giving pain meds in between. I also had to test the urine of all the diabetic patients before breakfast and lunch, which involved counting drops of urine into a test tube, dropping a Clinitest tablet into the urine, timing the reaction, and comparing the color to a

chart. This would determine the dose of insulin for some of these patients. This also was state of the art, long before personal blood glucose testing. Diabetes incidence here then was 3.7 times the national rate, per Rosebud tribal statistics.

I finally walked out of the med room into the hall with my tray of meds all organized. However, Vonnie our beloved unit clerk had set up a fan for the 107-degree August day, and there went all my little med cards flying across the hall. Morning meds were a bit late that day, despite my best efforts.

For the patients that we were unable to save, the hospital did have a morgue. It was in the creepy basement of our condemned and, some said, haunted building. We would bathe, wrap and tag the body, and wheel it down to the basement. There were two cooler doors with rolling trays, each to accommodate one body. However, due to the remoteness of the location, lack of phones and transportation, there might be delays in locating the next of kin, or in making funeral arrangements, so there were times when we had to double up the bodies on the slabs. Nice.

We also frequently had overcrowding with the live patients. Often the rooms were all full and patients were admitted to beds in the hallways. Tuberculosis was rampant, roughly eight times the national rate, and many of the patients in the hall beds should have been on isolation precautions, had the resources only been available. We gave TB skin tests to all patients as they were admitted to test their exposure. But they often didn't stay the two to three days necessary to read the outcome of the test, so there was no record of it being positive (or negative). They probably all wondered why their arms were swollen and itchy when they went home. If a patient had been previously exposed to TB and had had prior skin tests, the reaction caused the injection site to redden, swell and itch even more with each skin test.

Not only did patients have the discomfort of an irritated arm, but many went with undiagnosed and untreated active tuberculosis in the lungs, as well as advanced complications in the brain, spine, bones, and kidneys. The public health staff of two nurses was too small and homes were too remote to follow up on the test results. Even if we had told the patients who left before the test was read to contact us if their arm reacted, they likely would not have found a phone or a ride for something so minor as an irritated arm. In a remote land with only a few phones and cars, coming to the hospital was a major ordeal for most.

Eventually a hospital administrator had the brilliant idea to put a cap on the hospital census, so that when the beds in the rooms were full, we could no longer admit more patients to the hall. At least then everyone was in a room with some privacy and sanitation. I suppose that those who would have been admitted to the hall beds were either sent home or to another hospital, at least fifty miles away. Some of our patients were discharged earlier to make room for sicker folks coming in.

Sometimes we had to transport patients that weren't deemed sick enough to warrant the cost of the specialized Zipper Lady. Besides transporting Quannah Crow Dog on my first day of work, weeks later I was assigned to accompany a 14- year-old girl who was about 6 months pregnant with twins and in labor as she was airlifted to Denver. I monitored her vital signs and contractions and tried to keep her calm. But again, my main strategy was prayer. I really had no equipment or expertise to handle the situation if she should deliver two premature babies during the flight. I felt I was in way over my head, as usual. We did get her to Denver safely, but a couple of days later they sent her back to Rosebud, saying it had been false labor! I never heard what happened to her after that, though I wondered from time to time. Did she get sent out again? Did she give up on the hospital and deliver at home with a midwife or a medicine man? How did her babies do? I didn't see her in the hospital on any of my shifts.

Rosemarie had her own excitement transporting a pregnant woman. As she tells it,

"The doctor suspected the young mother was in early stages of labor with a pending breech delivery. He thought there was enough time to fly her to Rapid City for delivery and asked me to be the escort. Just before leaving the emergency room for the airstrip, the doctor asked if I had ever delivered a baby by breech. Of course, I hadn't! So, he gave me a thirty second lesson on breech delivery along with the emergency delivery kit and wished me good luck. The delivery kit was pretty basic, consisting of a basin, two towels, two umbilical clamps, sterile scissors, some gloves, and a baby blanket. But then, I thought maybe that's all that was needed. At the air strip I told the pilots that I wanted the patient's stretcher positioned in the plane with her head lower than her hips; I didn't want any pressure on her cervix. Thankfully a few hours later we arrived at Rapid City hospital with the mother still pregnant. I'm glad I didn't have to find out if I'd needed additional items in the delivery kit!"

The delivery kit was never offered to me on my transport, though I doubt it would have made a substantial difference with premature twins. I'm sure the Zipper Lady would have had a perfectly stocked delivery kit and skills to match.

Rosemarie relates another episode about a year later, in late summer of 1974:

"I had just gotten off the night shift and was looking forward to my day off. Of course, this meant that I was up for ambulance or flight escort if needed. In the late morning my phone rang and, sure enough, I was told that I was needed for an escort. The patient, in stable condition, was a high-ranking officer of AIM who had been shot by a state policeman. I was further told that FBI men were hiding in the hills surrounding the hospital, aiming their guns at the Indians who had surrounded the hospital with rifles in hand. The supervisor ended the call by telling me, 'Just walk in through the hospital doors like you know what you're doing.' I helped prepare the patient for transport and soon it was time to leave the hospital. I climbed inside through the back of the ambulance and took my position next to the patient. All along the ten-mile ride to the Mission air strip, Indians had lined the route, standing with their fists in the air just like in the Billy Jack movie. That was the longest ten-mile ride I ever had."

Sonny Waln was our usual ambulance driver, and we would give him money to bring back food for us from the McDonald's in Rapid City, about five hours away. Of course, by the time we got it, the food was cold and the fries were soggy, but it still tasted good to us, and as Dr. Tosi said, "It was exciting to spend money on something." Sonny wasn't always our driver though, and we had some other real doozies.

Stephanie was another young newly- graduated nurse from Maryland, who had arrived in Rosebud a few weeks before us. She was tall and distinguished by her remarkable curly chestnut-brown hair, freckles, nervous energy, and hearty laugh. She had arranged for a couple of days off after having her four wisdom teeth pulled. Alas, she had not arranged to leave town to recuperate. She got a desperate call begging her go on an ambulance run to take a man with internal injuries from a drunk driving accident to the Rapid City Hospital, 350 miles round trip. She tried to decline, but of course there was nobody else who could go. The man needed surgery, but Rosebud's surgeon was not available. Steph recalls this story:

"We'd already had to stop once at a local hospital along the way to restart the IV that the patient had pulled out while thrashing around the back of the ambulance. He had required sedation, which needed a doctor's order. The ambulance had then gotten a couple of hours beyond Rosebud when the driver said he had to pull over and take a nap! I looked at him like he had two heads and said, "You can't do that! We have to get this patient there in a hurry!" The driver replied that he was hung over and really could not stay awake and proceeded to park at the side of the road and pass out.

"We were in the middle of nowhere in the middle of the night. I still had chipmunk cheeks from the wisdom teeth extractions and cotton packing. I shoved the driver into the passenger seat, hopped into the driver's seat, and drove off to Rapid City at 80 mph, as there were no speed limits. I was driving with my left hand, looking back to check the IV, and to swat with my right hand at the patient, who was also drunk but thrashing around again, and to yell for him to lie back down! As we were approaching Rapid City, I had to wake up the driver to find the hospital, plus I was concerned that a special drivers' license might be required to drive the ambulance. Several hours later we returned from that wild ride and I went thankfully back to my own sick bed."

We all took our turns transporting patients, and Judy had the most memorable flight as "part of her orientation." She was assigned to bring an older woman named Mable back from Omaha, Nebraska where she'd been treated after suffering a stroke in Rosebud. As Judy tells it:

"The patient had reached maximum function and needed to come home. Well how exciting. Air transport. Wow. Yeah, well I'd heard some stories and thought I was braced for the challenge… First of all, arriving at the take-off point I saw the small

single engine plane on a strip of asphalt that ended in the town dump. But I got into the two-seater and off we went. The pilot was very quiet on the trip so I didn't learn much about this Antelope Air Service. We landed in Omaha about 3PM. It was immediately obvious that Mabel was not there and ready for transport. This annoyed the pilot, so he called to find out where she was. As time passed and no Mabel, he began to pace and look at his watch. His increasing anxiety was very noticeable.

"Finally, Mabel arrived on a stretcher. She was loaded into the back of the plane, with her head between the pilot's seat and mine. She was unable to talk. I checked vital signs and off we went heading west, back to Rosebud, in total silence with a very tense pilot. Finally, I couldn't take it any longer and asked what the problem was. I probably shouldn't have asked, because the answer wasn't something I wanted to hear. Daylight was fading and there was only one light on the plane. On top of that, there were no lights at the landing site! No lights! Now there were two anxious people flying west in silence. Since the Mission airfield was secluded by the dump, the blue bulbs were regularly shot out, and now were not being replaced! As the world faded to dark, the little plane continued heading west until all of a sudden, the pilot broke his silence and said, 'I think we're here.' Well exactly where was 'here'? No lights. Anywhere. And suddenly, 'Hold on,' and down we dived. The sudden dive had me bracing for a crash, and then we were heading back up. Level off. Check Mabel. And now we were well aware of what she had had for supper. Mixed vegetables, all back in full view, and I was sweeping her mouth to try and prevent her from aspirating the food into her lungs. Just as I thought we had stabilized, down we went again. No crash, and up again.

Talk about a roller coaster without a track, as the pilot continued his search in the dark for the runway. And then it happened. Two headlights from a truck went on below us. That's it! Our landing site! And down we went again. Never was there such a welcome feeling than bumpy bump bump as we rolled along the ground, then stopped. The plane had missed the runway and made a bumpy but safe landing in a field. Thank you, God! However, the ambulance was not there to bring the patient the last ten miles to the hospital. The guys asked me if I wanted to wait, and I said, 'No Way! We're not waiting!' They brought Mable and me the final distance to the hospital in the back of a station wagon. We'd survived my nursing orientation."

Another triumph of Rosebud ingenuity over desperation. And all without the Zipper Lady's

nifty gadgets. We'd all been thrown into the deep end and somehow managed the challenges, so far…

Woohitike.

Five Poems
Ed Schwartz

Hamlet at Red Bank

1.

Nothing sticks.

The paint, watered
runs down the wall.

2.

When it's over
the following
(cross the stage):

"Ophelia"

(a stagehand)

the "Hamlet" himself.

Town Clock

At noon
a god
emerges
pauses
wobbles
(a little)
then returns

Our Old Sack

the bottom

falling

out.

This White Air

I-M-M-E-N-S-E

Children of Aquarius

Some things became magical to us. For instance that street light near Millie's, where we stood one summer night…Millie, Les, Jeffery and me. And that little space became our stage, and we … the Children of Aquarius.

They were wrapped in each other's arms, Les and Millie (totally naked) their door open. And he called her Goose … and kissed her feet (Why didn't I leave?) and began sucking one breast, and then the other.

It was Millie's birthday. And we all dropped by. And Millie baked cupcakes. (Cute, Les called them) And Jeffery played the guitar. Calvin came. And even Barbara Scott (a friend from work).

My ass is enormous, Millie said. And Les kissed it. It's gigantic. No, Les said…it's adorable.

We went to the park. Les picked up a rock, looking for lizards. He found one. He held it up, and Millie wanted to see its color change. That's a chameleon, Les said. And placed it (gently) on the ground.

They were making up … again. You don't love me. I do! Buzzard-bait! Dolt! Pothead! Geek!

She fell off her ladder (and into my arms) her breasts on my wrists, (so warm) squealing with delight, the wall of their new Bronx apartment still half-painted. Imbecile, Les shouted (from up high).

Claudine (Millie's friend) came over. With her "feathers." And "beads."

Millie was pouting. (her lip out) Is my Cinderella sad, Les asked. But she continued pouting. You Orangutan, she said. And he kissed her nose.

And then everything changed. It all seemed so "different" (suddenly), that "refuge," that "fairyland" (they lived in). I couldn't explain it. I left one day … and never went back.

Cabrón

Ken Kakareka

I stuck out like a clean sock in a dirty pile. I lived in DT Fullerton, on the other side of the bridge, a neighborhood called "Little Mexico." One street over, Valencia, was known for gang violence. This Finnish woman and I were the only white people who lived in the neighborhood. Our apartment complex was on a residential street across from industrial buildings and the railroad tracks. The house next door used to be a drug house with a Pitbull, but my landlord said it was no longer a drug house. It still had the Pitbull. Two houses down, on the corner, was a house of Cholos. They blared Banda music all day and night with all kinds of stuff in the front yard for sale, like a mini-swap meet. I'm not sure what kind of operation they were running.

Jasper by Tom Driscoll

I was dating a girl from the neighborhood named Rosario. Her dad hated me. He was a decent man but a religious lunatic. The first time I ever went over, he didn't lift his head from the Bible. He already knew that I was white. God damn, I thought. We're in California, not Texas. Us wetos only look like we want to build the wall—we don't actually want to build it! It didn't matter though. Rosario's dad already made up his mind about who he wanted his daughter to date. It wasn't a white boy.

The next time Rosario came over, I sent her home with a bunch of hickeys all over her neck. Big glistening things.

"You can't do that," said Carlos, a friend from my building. "He's gonna' kill you!"

"Relax," I said. "It's all good."

But it wasn't all good. The next time I went over, Rosario's dad stood up from the Bible as I walked in.

"Sir," I said, extending a hand.

"What in God's name do you think you're doing?"

"Don't get God involved," I said. He turned red as a tamale and flipped the table. Before I knew it, I saw stars before my eyes.

I woke up to Rosario and her mom pushing me in a stretcher. Her mom was a heavy-set woman—she had trouble keeping up. There were doctors, too. I glanced around at the walls, streaks of white. I put my head back down.

When I woke up again, I was in a room with Rosario and her mom. Her mom was crying and praying the rosary in Spanish. Rosario's dad was nowhere to be found. He was probably at home still reading the Bible. Rosario's hickeys were starting to fade. I'd have to freshen them up next time she came over, I thought.

"Can I get you anything, mi amor?" she asked, tenderly trembling. I shook my head and smiled. "My dad can be such an *asshole* sometimes, I hate him!" He was an overgrown man-child – it was true. One time, we were all at Easter mass, and he sat in his own pew refusing to sit with Rosario, her mom, and me in another pew. Rosario and her mom cursed him in Spanish the entire mass calling him a stubborn mule.

Rosario's mom cried out from the corner of the room. I must've been a ghastly site, because her hands were shaking and her face was scrunched like a crushed grape. Tears were streaming at an unprecedented rate. Rosario walked over to her mom, helped her out of the room, and came back in. She held a mirror in front of my face so that I could see it. I *was* a ghastly site, indeed. Something in between the elephant man and Stephen Hawking – a physical deformity. I had this lopsided bandage around my head covering a lump above my left eyebrow. The whole left side of my face drooped from my eye down, like Bell 's Palsy. Rosario told me her dad wacked me a couple times with the spine of the Bible. Then he used his fist. I had to get 20 stitches above my eyebrow. It was going to be a hefty hospital bill for Jesus' disciple.

The doctor came in and gave us the rundown. I had to ice my face, clean the wounds, and come back in a couple weeks to have the stitches removed. He asked what happened and laughed when I told him about it. The doc looked old enough to have a daughter Rosario's age – I wanted to find her and give her a bunch of hickeys, too. He probably would react the same way Rosario's dad did, and I'd never leave the hospital.

After the doctor left, Rosario went back out to check on her mom. She was in the little chapel at the end of the hall, kneeling before Christ. So many prayers probably couldn't save me or her husband at this point. I didn't know who she was praying for more.

Rosario came back in and told me she was worried about her mom's anxiety. She wondered if, since they were at the hospital, maybe her mom should get some tests done. "No, mi amor," I said. "I can't stay any longer at this hospital." She smiled and understood. She pulled the curtain over and started kissing, biting, and pushing her tongue into my mouth. Then her hand brushed my wood and I didn't stop it. When I moved my hand up her leg and squeezed a cheek, she swatted it away and laughed.

Luckily, the incident happened on a Friday night, so I didn't have to take time off from work. I had the weekend to recuperate. Rosario came over and took care of me on Saturday. On Sunday, she had to go work the swap meet in the morning, but she came over that night. I gave her some hickeys, but only on her breasts—she couldn't resist them.

The next time I went over for dinner, Rosario's dad didn't come to the table. He stayed in his bedroom, and the three of us ate in silence while his plate sat there getting cold. I almost asked to eat it but resisted the temptation to be an asshole. Rosario's mom gave me seconds anyway. The gall, her dad probably thought, for me to show up at his house again. The only time I saw him that night was when he stuck his head out the bathroom window and told Rosario it was time for me to go. She and I were sitting on a swing chair in her back yard, playing with the dogs. They had four of them. "Hi sir," I called to him. But he slammed the window shut and Rosario walked me out to my car.

All of Rosario's other family members liked me. Her mom, Tias and Tios, cousins, and the dogs. I went to family gatherings, trips, everything, and everyone talked and laughed with me, and not with her dad. He wasn't a social butterfly anyway – a rather dull and lifeless creature. I think it made him sick to see everyone take to me. I was an avocado from the tree he could not shake. I just kept coming around.

Usually, when I went to the house, he avoided me and acted like I didn't exist. Sometimes, we would exchange a handshake "hello" and "good-bye," but that was the extent of it. Often, if it was night time, it ended with him getting up and shutting off the T.V. even if Rosario and I were in the middle of a movie. He'd go to the kitchen table with his Bible and that was my cue to leave. Rosario and her mom would get so embarrassed that they'd both walk me out and apologize for his behavior.

One night, the first time he tried to initiate conversation was when he asked Rosario if her and I wanted to join him at the table for the Bible. It wasn't so much a conversation as it was a reading. He read first in Spanish and then I read the same passage in English. Then he read again. The second time he read was much longer than the first—maybe 7 or 8 pages. The print in the Bible is very tiny. During that segment, Rosario and I got hand-sy with each other underneath the table. She moved her hand up my thigh, and I had to swat it away. This time she was the cabróna. After the reading, her dad proceeded to give us a lecture in broken English, some in Spanish, about chastity. The whole thing was very queer—Rosario was a grown woman, almost 30.

I took trips with the entire family to San Juan Capistrano, to the mountains, the beaches, even to Vegas. Rosario's dad didn't go to Vegas—we went for one of her cousin's baby's christening. Vegas was too satanic a town for him. Celebrations in Mexican culture for Baptisms are not for children, they are for adults. There was an open bar, and all of us got drunk. I twirled Rosario's mom around the dance floor in honor of her husband's absence. All of her Tias praised me after that. It was a milestone with her family because I broke some ground with her Tios, too. They were stand-offish up until that weekend, but we talked about construction and drank Corona.

I went to birthday parties and holiday gatherings—Rosario and I were even asked to be the godparents at one of her younger cousin's Quinceañera. That particular Tia, the mother of the girl, was my favorite family member, the one I was closest to.

Eventually, Rosario's dad initiated minor talk at the dinner table. He even asked Rosario about my well-being and whereabouts on weeks when he hadn't seen me. Rosario told me about it. But there were encounters where he seemed cold and none of the headway mattered. "Ignore him," Rosario and her mom told me. He was a grown man going through menopause it seemed. The fluctuations in mood were astonishing.

Christmas came, and I went over the day before Christmas Eve because I was leaving. My family lived on the east coast, so I was going back to be with them for the holidays. I went over bearing gifts like a disciple of Jesus, trying to join her dad's team. First, I gave Rosario her gifts, and she opened them one by one. Bed sheets, a pair of Disney earrings, an old record player with poems I wrote on old records … a bunch of stuff both practical and sentimental. Then she read her card. Her cheeks flushed rose-colored, and she squeezed me and kissed me on the cheek.

"Feliz Navidad," I said, handing her parents their gifts, hugging her mom and shaking her dad's hand. Her dad opened his—a bland, navy cap from Marshalls that matched him, similar to one I'd seen him wear around the house. He wore them for yard work so I figured he could use a new one, since the old one was all dingy and stained. Rosario translated the message on the card for him. "… *I admire how well you take care of your family … Enjoy your family on Jesus' birthday … God Bless …*" He smiled when she was done reading it. "Thank you, man," he said. His eyes were a little moist, but it could've been his allergies.

Then Rosario's mom opened her gift and raised it in front of her face. It was a big, festive wreath frosted and decorated with bells, ribbons, and a variety of fake nuts and dried fruits. Rosario sat next to her and translated the card. "… *Thank you for everything, accepting me into your family … Your spirit is beautiful and vibrant … You are a wonderful mother and wife … Feliz Navidad …*" She lowered the wreath and her face was a wet, scrunched grape again, like at the hospital, but this time joyous. Rosario's dad thanked me and shook my hand again. "Have a good time with your family," he said. He wished them a Merry Christmas and a happy new year.

That night, her dad let me stay as late as I wanted to. It was a major breakthrough.

From there on out, he was civil. The mood fluctuations remained, but I realized he wasn't just an asshole to me, but to everyone. Just to me a little more. Rosario and I had to capitalize on the days when he was pleasant. It was about 20% to 80%. What I mean by capitalize is that we had to take advantage of his delightful moods. For instance, one night Rosario and I had plans to get Indian food, ice cream, and go see a movie. We decided to scrap that, because her mom was grilling chicken, and her dad asked us if we were joining them for dinner. He was drinking Modelo (something he did about twice a year but could've benefited more from). Since I'd seen him smile more in that one night than ever before, we couldn't say no. Rosario

and I ran out to Stater Bros. to get some buns and more Modelo.

At dinner, it was the most her dad ever tried to talk to me. He asked about my family and Philadelphia. I asked about his family and Guadalajara. He didn't offer me any Modelo, but it was ok because it was shit anyway. I drank some of Rosario's mom's home-made sweet tea instead. The mutts were under the table begging for food the whole dinner, so we fed them scraps, but they only begged for more. The youngest one, Rocky, a little Doberman pincher, was a little cabrón. They were always calling him one. He jumped up onto Rosario's lap and knocked a drink out of her hand all over her shirt. Both her and her mom scolded the dog, and her mom chased him away with a stick. Rosario took off her wet shirt, wearing only a tank top underneath. Her bosoms flared, and big, glistening marks revealed themselves, like treasure, all over her chest. They started right below her neck and gleamed down her lumps to where her dad couldn't see any more. His eyes widened—the same marks he had seen on Rosario's neck were now on her breasts. His fork clashed against his plate, and he exploded out of his chair like a rocket.

"You fucking puta!" he said. "Get out of my house!" He turned red as a tamale and transformed from one of Jesus' disciples into the devil.

I saw the table flip, the stretcher, her mom's prayers, and the bandages again. Not again. I left before any of that could happen. Rosario and her mom (crying) followed me out of the house. It was going to be a long comeback from this one to Jesus' disciple.

Three Poems
Marcus Hines

Fictitious

Fictitious, she is, amber is the shade of her iris
I carry the scent of her with me or so I want to believe
That it still lingers on my lips. But in truth, she's always out of my reach
It all began with a lucid dream of the highlands, wind dancing through the fields like a symphony
As if she conducted it herself. Until the sun set behind her
Casting a silhouette that gently blanketed the hills
All was covered except a house with fractured brick and forlorning steel
The door is of rotting sycamore, broken picture frames and damaged window panes welcomed me inside
Closely, I was running my hands along each crevice of the walls, digging out chips of lavender from beneath
     the skin of my palms
It was dark, but all too familiar as I made my way towards the kitchen, where there is a mahogany table
Only to ever be accompanied by cobwebs and a candle. Smoke stained glass was scattered like pieces of a
     puzzle
Perfectly symmetrical across the floor. I walked atop it with bare feet, it never drew blood
But deeply left a scar. From the bedroom, my full name being called
Where the shadows slowly took form, to fill in the curves of a woman
Biting the scarlet dipped nail of her thumb. Moonlit skin, her hair was kissed by the ocean sand
That was cascading near endlessly over her spine. I tell myself this is fiction, but I bring myself here every
     time
To the exact moment I found myself hers, but she'll never be mine

Midnight Hours

Another morning of waking up to dial tones that seem perpetual
Churned guts carry a soul that feels woven in between forlorn steel
All stemming from a dream, I was scaling the pearly gates but rust has corroded all the gold
I saw you on the other side trying to catch your breath, holding tightly to an old rosary until your skin began
     to peel
When I awoke, cigarette burns and wine stained screen-doors tell a story of the midnight hours
But I ever so ungracefully steadied my limbs and made it home
Just maybe my angels have their fingers crossed or hell has indeed frozen and has no vacancy
Nevertheless, I tend to always find myself searching for your voice on the receiving end of this phone
Before I close my weary eyes and rest these bitter bones, contemplating if I should mend or grieve
From dusk to dawn, your aesthetic still gently lingers like a counterfeit silhouette

And it comforts me more than the countless threads that make up this tattered bed
Give up, give in, I forfeit, I'm drawn to you like a weathered anchor in a violent sea
Tending to your memory like a treasured garden, but all that buds is plagued with disdain
Harvesting precious moments while the winds roar as a constant, never to secede
One day may I hope to find refuge from this mischievous, vicious, love

Purpose

There's a vulture perched upon the surface of your heart
Digging deep with jagged talons, never leaving you to scar
It whispers to me, gathering a bouquet of bones
Regardless of the pleas, there'll never be enough love here for us both
And if you let me, dear, I can pluck it from your chest
Just concentrate on the subtle spaces between breaths
That is where I'll be
There's a serpent coiled inside your throat
Shedding countless shades, before it causes you to choke
I'll brave the rapids of your veins, and climb atop your lungs
And if you let me, dear, I can unravel this mess behind your tongue
Just concentrate on the grey before morning comes
That is where I'll be
There are teeth along the pivots of your soul
And they sink into my arms the harder that I hold
With calloused hands I will carefully cascade down your spine
And if you let me, dear, this madness I will bind
Just concentrate on the wounds that no longer bleed
That is where I'll be
You are my purpose

The Dog Days of Winter
Ken Fliés

From Into the Backlands, a Lost Lake Folk Art memoir scheduled to be released in September 2018.

A Peace Corps Memoir

I read once that the phrase "dog days of summer" originated with the ancient Romans. Back home, the dog days ran from mid-July and lasted at least a month—supposedly the period of least rainfall in the Midwest, and the hottest, sultriest days of summer.

In Brazil, however, it was winter and there had been no rain for several months. The landscape was brown and dry with trees stripped bare. Dust clung to every building and tree, and the roads were little more than pools of dust. There was no feed on the land for cattle; they became skinny, sullen wretches whose every rib bone could be counted, the fortunate ones already sent to slaughter.

Not only did plant and animal life suffer, but languor seemed to be the state of people as well. The air was hot and asphyxiating and the humidity low. It could drop to as low as ten to fifteen percent, causing a lot of

Peace Corps Volunteer Ken Fliés on a river ferry in Brazil, 1962.

respiratory problems. The town seemed to have passed from existence. People stayed indoors out of the heat and dust for fear of contracting the *gripe*—flu, so there was little activity on the streets. Truly, the dog days had arrived.

It was indeed the dog days of winter for our old dog Pluto. Shortly after returning from our travels we went to Santa Maria for a couple days to rewire their water pumping station with materials we obtained on our trip. Usually upon arriving home at any time of day or night, Pluto would come running from behind the house to greet us; not this time. Our neighbor João Amador came over and told us that Paulo (Dr. Pepper II) had come by late the day before with a rifle and shot Pluto. João said he noticed Pluto was foaming at the mouth and having trouble with his balance, so they assumed he had rabies. A rabies bite in the backlands meant death, nothing else.

This was truly the most depressing time of the year in Brazil and I found myself engrossed often in beautiful memories of home to overcome the morass of it all. While Minnesota winters can be harsh—temperatures averaged eleven degrees in the winter of 1962-1963, with many days failing to climb above zero—there is also contrast and beauty winters produce, which is not found in the stark Brazilian landscape; no day-to-day change for months. When long Midwest winters ultimately abate, they produce a phenomenon known as spring fever and a time of new beginnings.

It gradually dawned on me that another beautiful spring and summer back home would pass before I returned to my family and my sweetheart waiting for me. My journey had become more emotionally trying over time, but it was never more difficult than when I realized I still had a long road ahead.

Feeling somehow responsible for the death of old Pluto, João managed to find a younger replacement for us a few weeks later. When he brought the dog by he told us that they had named it *Duque*—Duke. At first, I thought this was quite an honor. This was the revered title given to only one person, possibly the greatest Brazilian leader of all times: Luiz Alves de Lima e Silva, *Duque de Caxias*—Duke of Boxes. The Duke fought in the War of Independence in Brazil and led Brazilian forces in the Ragamuffin War, the Platine War against Argentina, and in the bloody Paraguay War. He subsequently became a baron, a count, a marquis, and finally the only person ever titled a duke during the reign of the King Pedro II in Brazil. John Wayne had nothing over this guy.

In Portuguese, I told João that having the name of the famous Duque de Caxias for the dog was quite an honor, thinking he would be duly impressed with my knowledge of Brazilian history. João, who did not speak English, shook his head and said, "*Não, sabe Duque in Inglês,*"—No, Duque. Well, we knew *Duque* in English was Duke, but after he repeated it a few more times we came to understand that he was trying to say "doggie." Apparently João had asked someone who knew a little English how to properly refer to a canine. After the rabies scare with old Pluto, neither Dick nor I were especially crazy about the idea of having another dog. Once we realized that we were not treading on sacred ground, and the animal was just a doggie and not the reincarnation of the famous

Duke, we told João as politely as possible we would be honored to have him name it Doggie, but it would be best to leave the dog in the care of his young daughter, who had already become fondly attached to it.

Dog days or not, there was work to be done. In addition to our usual workday responsibilities, the school term was underway. I had promised Padre that I would teach evening classes in English, math, and some history and geography. Although not a teacher by any stretch of my imagination, one year of college in the United States (the equivalent of a master's degree for a teacher in Correntina) put me at the top of the faculty.

Like most small towns in America, the font of local gossip and insight into political correctness was the local barbershop. It was no different in Correntina. The barbershop was also the gathering place for local sages and pundits. We came to refer to them as the barbershop boys. During the Festival of the Divine, the barbershop boys assumed we would find a young woman to our liking among all the virgins.

Right on the heels of all the dog days holidays I decided maybe the best thing to do was to hightail it out of town before something else delayed our work. While we had lots of mechanical projects on our plate, I was determined not to lose sight of my agricultural plans. With this in mind, I headed for the commission agricultural station at the Formoso Colony on the Formoso River some fifty miles away to visit my old soccer nemesis, Wilson.

Arriving in the colony, I was met with pandemonium. Evidently a wildcat had somehow entered the compound the previous night and stolen a couple pigs. Therefore, the day was consumed with improving fencing and pens and discovering who was at fault for not locking up the pigs. The theft had occurred on Sunday, and Wilson said it most likely involved someone drinking a little too much cachaça the night before and nodding off on the job.

During my visit, Wilson did his best to convince me to move there to work with him. This was very tempting as they had a tractor and other equipment I did not have, and I enjoyed Wilson's company. Fortunately, other Volunteers were coming in a month or two as part of the Brazil III project and they would be stationed in and around Santa Maria, including at the colony. Wilson was wondering if I would simply just trade places with his designated new arrival since he still had soccer on his mind. But why take the chance? The new Volunteer might not be an athlete.

The next day Wilson asked if I would drive to Lapa to pick up Dr. Giovanni, a government official working with settling landless peasants. Upon arriving back in the colony with Dr. Giovanni, we had a most interesting meeting with a group of peasants, each of whom was slated to receive a free forty-acre plot of land from the federal government. Several conditions were attached, one of which was to provide proof of identity in the form of a birth record, marriage license, or some other official document. None of them could produce any of these documents.

The peasants were assigned numbered plots and needed to write down the number. But few among them could write, and those who could write, wrote a number between one and ten, even though there were forty lots assigned. This created considerable confusion and led to heated arguments over who had been assigned which lot. Names did not help since many of them had common names, and some did not know their surnames. Another condition dealt with house restrictions, such as prohibiting the building of a pigpen next to a home since this was a common practice and one of the chief sources of disease among the rural poor. People did this primarily to keep a close eye on the pigs and protect them from marauding thieves such as the wildcats, as well as foxes and even humans.

One of the more intelligent landless fellows took serious umbrage at this condition and got in an intense argument with Drs. Giovanni and Wilson. In frustration, he finally turned to me and asked if we had to do this in the United States. I proceeded to tell him that indeed we had to build our pigpens some distance from our houses. It seemed that he had heard the United States was the land of the free and we could do pretty much as we pleased. While he did not want to listen to or believe the good doctors, somehow my position on the matter made sense to him and he agreed to build the pen away from the house.

We assured him that we would supply wire mesh fence instead of the flimsier but typical woven stick fence and that he could erect it to a sufficient height to keep out marauding animals. When this intelligent chap asked me how Americans prevented intruders, I told him we used fencing that had a current passing through it called an electric fence. He wondered if this fence would keep out marauding human thieves. I replied that if enough electricity was run through the wire it would not only keep them out of the pen, it would kill them. He and the others loved this idea.

I noticed Dr. Wilson just smiling and shaking his head, and I knew maybe I had taken this a step too far. Wilson informed them that although no such innovation was planned, the colony would get electricity in the near future from our hydro complex in Correntina. For now, they would just have to take turns sitting up at night to guard the pigs. After a week's time, I headed back home. Wilson would not let me bring his only functioning tractor to Correntina, but he promised to do what he could to help find some seeds and other things I desired.

We signed the lease for a house located in town on the village square, the church only twenty yards from our front door, and the town and county offices right next to the church. Diagonally across the square was the market, and right across the river sat the saw mill, Padre's rectory, the school where I would be teaching, and Padre's farm with horses.

The house had been vacant for some time and needed a lot of work. It lacked water, electricity, a toilet or shower, and furnishings. The roof leaked when it rained, and it had only a wood burning stove to cook on. So that was the bad news. The good news was we rented it for a whopping five dollars a month. The additional good news was that the house had a large back yard that I hoped to turn into a greenhouse. The additional bad news was that the yard had formerly been used as a horse corral, and there was a dilapidated building at the end of the alley that would have to be disassembled. At least the yard was protected by a wall, so I wouldn't have to worry about chickens or dogs destroying the fruits of my labor.

Given all the work required, the structure presented an excellent opportunity to create a multipurpose project: repair and upgrade the house while training locals in the practical trades of plumbing, electrical wiring, and carpentry. Even finer woodworking skills could be taught since we needed beds, bookshelves, a table or two, and benches to sit on.

These dog days of winter made it a good time of the year to be doing this work. It had cooled down slightly, enough to cause the locals to wake me up one night and come outside. They wanted to know if what was happening in the air was what we called snow, but it turned out to be a rare bout of fog. The dry, dusty conditions induced hibernation throughout town. Fewer people came to the market since there was less to sell, with most land fallow and livestock nothing but skin and bones. Many of the students my age were away at school, so social activity was also at low ebb.

The only big social event that winter was the marriage of the mayor's son to Yvonne Coimbra. Sometime earlier, Adherbal and Yvonne had asked me to be the best man for their civil wedding ceremony. This turned out to be the social event of the season if not the year, but I didn't bring much for fancy clothes along to Brazil. Keno, a brother-in-law of the Comibra's, was the town's tailor and he was willing to make a suit for me. We spent a lot of time selecting just the right fabric, the best in town. Keno wanted perfect results to the point of going beyond the old carpenter rule of measure twice and cut once. His fastidious approach yielded a gorgeous suit and an exquisite fit. I told Keno there was only one thing missing. He asked me what that was. I told him I could not find the tailor's label *Keno of Correntina*.

He laughed loudly but I said, "I plan on taking this to Rio, Salvador, and even to America with me. When folks see this, you will be the rival of Oleg Cassini and Pierre Cardin!"

Whether or not my compliment made any difference, I am not sure, but Keno did not charge me for the suit.

The grand wedding took place as planned with leading citizens from Correntina and the surrounding towns present. Dr. Oswaldo, Correntina's new and first-ever county prosecutor, performed the ceremony. As best man, I was required to sign the marriage certificate. Dr. Oswaldo said this posed a complication since the certificate would be the first legal document in the county ever signed by someone not born in Brazil. After checking with state officials, he eventually found a way it could be done—quite an honor for me all the same.

The barbershop boys reported that some of the ladies in town who followed American movie stars featured in Brazilian magazines said Dr. Oswaldo was a spitting image of the famous American actor Clark Gable. I agreed they had a valid point. He had the little mustache, jet-black hair, and was indeed a handsome dude. The boys said they thought his presence would take the pressure off Dick and me, but especially off me after women saw me in my fancy new suit.

Since we had the only hardtop Jeep in town, it became the official wedding vehicle for the newlyweds and bridesmaids. Dick chauffeured, even without a suit. When people did something in Brazil that was not proper or up to standards, they were chided with the words *sem vergonha*. Interpreted, this can take on several nuances ranging from shameless, disgraceful, or scandalous to the point of mortification. The barbershop boys, although not a pernicious lot but prone to frivolity, jokingly told Dick he was *sem vergonha* and they would chip in to buy him a suit before the next big event rolled around.

As time progressed we saw less of our project management personnel, in spite of our various project problems, significant attrition, and the country teetering on the brink of a revolution. One reason for this was expansion. The Peace Corps had several new projects groups training for Brazil, a full seven that would grace the country before our project terminated. The first of these, deemed Brazil III, had just arrived and been stationed in the valley, boosting the number of Volunteers to six assigned downriver from Correntina at Santa Maria, Santana, and the Formoso Colony. Among these new Volunteers were a skyscraper builder from New York, an Alaskan commercial fisherman, and a pipe-smoking cowboy from Texas.

Upon their arrival, I traveled to their locations to orient them to their new surroundings. The new Volunteer stationed in the colony was the commercial fisherman named Rick, so I took him and the Texan to introduce them to Drs. Giovanni and Wilson. I knew Wilson's primary interest in my coming to the colony was to play on his Santa Maria soccer team against their hated rivals in

Correntina. I had previously declined, figuring that the new prospects would most likely be good athletes. I noticed Wilson assessing pint-sized Rick and the lanky, bow-legged Texan. I think he felt that, while these two Volunteers may have possibly excelled at fishing and bareback rodeo riding, soccer was not likely their forte. I gave Wilson a wink of the eye and he returned a giant but shy smile. Sometimes a gift does not contain everything you wish for.

Not long after our new colleagues arrived, we drove to Lapa to meet some of the other new Volunteers and to take in the largest annual area event, which was the celebration of the day the priest who lived in the cave with a cougar supposedly saw the image of Christ. August sixth also marked the Catholic holy day of the Transfiguration. A miracle reported in the New Testament, Jesus underwent metamorphosis while praying on a mountain, and became radiant with glory. It amazed me that in Lapa there was a big rock—a mountain—and inside the mountain, in a grotto, a priest living with a cougar reputedly saw the image of Jesus. What a coincidence.

During this event, the town swelled from a population of 10,000 to more than 100,000 pilgrims. Hordes of people gathered along the river reminded me of photos of the Ganges River in India in an old encyclopedia I stored under my bed back home. People bathed and washed their clothes in the river, and most likely it provided their source of drinking water and served as a latrine. With the throngs of souls gathered, the President decided it was a good time to visit the region. The original purpose of a presidential visit was to officially inaugurate the hydro dam in Correntina, but government officials visited Correntina and decided against that plan. Perhaps they wanted to avoid the donkeys and the cotton gin on our so-called airstrip. Whatever the case, they decided to the chagrin of the locals that if an inaugural switch was to be thrown, it would be done in Lapa.

The Brazilian President went by the nickname Jango. My fellow project Volunteer, Airman Jim in Lapa, wrote the following passages about Jango's visit and our encounter with him: "A gathering of locals collected outside my house awaiting the President's arrival. After a meeting with the Commission Chief Dr. Lascarus, President Goulart was escorted on foot to the meeting place, leading the entourage himself. As he approached head down, looking neither left nor right, I and another Volunteer, Ken Fliés, impulsively stepped out with our hands extended to greet the President, saying in Portuguese, 'Bom dia Senhor Presidente. Muito Prazer—Good day Mr. President. It is a pleasure to meet you.

"With undisguised indifference, he raised his head cautiously and gave us the once-over. Being unable to ignore our outstretched hands, he replied by nodding slightly and giving us in return a limp, damp hand to shake that felt like cold fish and, without a word, continued on his way. His bodyguards, no doubt taken aback by our effrontery, had made no effort to intervene."

During the afternoon festivities, Jango's itinerary called for a visit to the holy site. Inside the cave, stalactites dripped water that was considered holy, plus there was an area called the Sala das Milagres— Room of Miracles. Given the tenuousness of Jango's presidency at the moment, he might have been looking for a miracle or two. Airman Jim observed Jango's march to the cave from the vantage point of a small plane joined by none other than our friend Reverend Reisner.

"We flew over the town, circling especially over the church plaza where Goulart would make another appearance. Below us in the narrow cobblestone streets leading to the cave and the plaza, thronged thousands of pilgrims. We circled at less than a thousand feet going round and round the hill, losing sight at times of the festivities. On about the fourth or fifth pass we saw the President's car drive up and then, on the next pass, we saw a column of smoke rising from the plaza and people running frantically away from the scene. Something awful had happened.

"We immediately thought there had been an attempt on the President's life and hurried to the airport. We soon learned that the smoke we had seen had been caused by a box of fireworks having blown up after a rocket misfired. A number of pilgrims were badly burned by the resulting explosion. The President was rushed to the airport and flown off in great haste. The injured were left to fend for themselves in a place where medical facilities were sorely lacking."

The getaway from Correntina was short but historic for us; for President Jango as well, I suspect. Jango no doubt understood his religion. The Feast of the Transfiguration was a celebration of Holy Trinity: God speaking from heaven, God the son being transfigured, the Holy Spirit present in the form of a cloud. The blast Jango had witnessed could be interpreted as a message from heaven. The transfigured son possibly represented the President's own life, and the cloud of smoke he had witnessed was the Holy Spirit telling him to get the hell out of Lapa. An astute historian, Jango might have remembered that not many years before on the Day of the Transfiguration, Hiroshima was leveled by an atomic bomb. Known in church circles as the Little Epiphany, the fireworks explosion was more than Jango cared to deal with in a backwater town like Lapa.

It was late afternoon before we could get a lift across the river, its banks lined with a massive tent city as far as one could see. When we got to Santa Maria, there were five trucks with pilgrims and a Jeep waiting for the muscle men to ferry them across the Formoso River, so it was ten-thirty in the dark of night before we made it across and midnight before we rolled into Correntina.

Well, it was back to the mill and to work on the house. I finished removing the structure from the back yard and continued building hotbeds for a greenhouse. We received a bonus with the new batch of Brazil III Volunteers. Two of them were roving mechanics who periodically relieved us of some of our mechanical workload, allowing us to focus more on the hydro installation and agriculture.

Soon after our return, director Leo paid us a short visit, this time with his lovely wife. Mrs. Leo apologized for not staying longer. She said, based on what she'd seen so far on her trip through the São Francisco Valley, that this was the prettiest place by far. She even chided Leo for not having done a better job of planning to stay the evening. And once she viewed my fabulous swimming pool, she reprimanded him all the more, saying if she'd known about the pool, she'd have brought her swimming suit. Perhaps to avert a family quarrel in our presence, Leo told her the five of us would all stand guard if she wanted to go for a quick skinny dip. It was a nice try but modesty won out.

Obviously there had been too much excitement surrounding the old swimming hole because within a short time, the canal sprung a leak in the cement wall. The floodgates had to be raised to lower the water in the canal below the crack and there would be no electricity for anyone for the next day or two while repairs were being made. This did not make for a village of happy campers. When the leak first occurred, we had images in our minds of the story the German had told us months earlier about the lack of the proper amount of cement and the collapsing hydro dams in Bolivia.

By now one year had passed since we had left our homes in America. It had been a year of incredible adventure and experience never to be forgotten. What better way to mark that milestone than by a special delivery I received in the mail about this time. It was addressed to me personally from the President of the United States of America:

The White House
Washington
July 29, 1963
Dear Mr. Flies:

You have recently completed your first year of service in the Peace Corps.

At home and abroad the Peace Corps has been recognized as a genuine and effective expression of the highest ideals and the best traditions of our Nation. You and your fellow Volunteers have made that judgment possible.

I am proud of your participation and I trust that in your second year of service your conduct and performance will continue to reflect credit upon you and the Peace Corps.

Sincerely,
John F. Kennedy

Waiting for the Prince
Nicole Borg

Nicole Borg's Up On Big Rock Poetry Series collection, *All Roads Lead Home,* was released in April 2018.

This is no fairy tale.
The man on the horse in the woods
is just as lost as you; he turns
the map in his hands and turns away.
So, pace the turret, if you must,
throw down your hair.
Wait, until your story's pages yellow,
the binding's leather cracks,
your thick locks gray.
Where the hell is he?

This is no once-upon-a-time.
The happy ending is as much a lie
as the prince. It's likely there
has never been a happy ending.
A kiss is a kiss—sweet. Sometimes
there are happy middles and
satisfying season finales.

The mirror shows just one reflection
and a lot depends on lighting.
Apples have a bad reputation
through no fault of their own.
Slippers of glass break or give you
blisters, or at the least, make your feet sweat.
The woodcutter had other options.
So do you.

Sisters, step-sisters, step-mothers—
the time is no more or less right
to be your own fairy godmother.
Cut off that prison of long hair.
Get a pair of traveling shoes
and your own mare. Wear chinos.
Leave the map in the tower.
Listen—the birds, the trees,
the wind that is beholden to no one.

Make a wish.
Then, make it happen.

Late Thoughts

Emilio DeGrazia

Emeritus Poet Laureate of Winona, Minnesota

I've always admired the honesty of Robert Frost's poem "The Road Not Taken." Frost's traveler comes to a fork in a forest path and confronts a choice. On a whim not based on logic or practicality he takes the road that seems "less travelled by," though the other is worn "about the same." Will his choice take him to some pleasant Walden Pond idyll, a more harmonious life in "Nature"? Frost, a farmer, was only occasionally charmed by "Nature," a tuft of flowers here or there. He had a dark philosophical view of nature, seeing clearly that it has death-designs on all of us. This dark design was on his mind when he concluded that "way leads on to way." He well understood that the chain reactions that result from the choices we make send us toward unknown futures and fates. And not only the unknown but death hangs silently over him as he, on a whim, "chooses" his path: "I doubted if I should ever come back."

Mayo Clinic St. Marys Hospital courtyard by Tom Driscoll

This thought becomes especially poignant when I'm suddenly sitting in the Mayo Clinic Emergency Room with something unknown going terribly wrong with my heart. The odd thing is that though I've arrived at a fork in my life journey, I'm powerless to avoid the limited options suddenly in play. In short, I'm looking at death as one of them. But it's very strange that from my bed everything seems everyday ordinary—the nurses and aides coming and going, the colors of the chairs and walls, the tops of trees swaying outside the windows to my left. The road not yet taken, death, is nowhere in sight. Out of sight and almost out of mind, with the question, "What next?" walking me backward down memory paths already well trod.

I've studied literature the better—the best—part of my life, and I've shown a prejudice for the darker, and tragic, narratives. Tragic heroes, unlike poor Oedipus as reigning king, usually die in those stories, and we close the book satisfied that this is how some personal histories rightly and of necessity conclude.

We learn, I think, best from them.

My studies also have taught me that a life well-lived requires a narrative worth living in. A self-story, a system or myth, provides a mental construct by which we can find order, direction, and meaning. Some of us align ourselves to traditional myths—the Christian story, for example—and find comfort and meaning in them. Those skeptical of traditional religions—I am one—are on their own to create their own. "I must create a system," said the poet William Blake, "or be enslaved by another man's."

Skepticism nags those who try to construct a story worth living in. The problem is complicated by the fact that we live in a sea of stories, many of them in conflict. And I don't want a story too narrow minded to represent me. I live in a community and nation and therefore have many complex ways of seeing myself as a character. It's hard for me to see myself as an American, peace lover, meat-eater and package of neurons, flesh and bones—all at the same time. And it's hard to prioritize my various identities. When I'm also expected to act out my roles as male, black, white, or "other," I often find myself conflicted or confused. I suspect we all live in strange, perhaps unprecedented, times. While "the spirit of the times" seems so whacky that the need to develop self-stories that stabilize us seems obvious, we are simultaneously asked to "deconstruct" the many narratives confusing us. As ancient scriptures about gender are being re-examined, "male" and "female" are no longer what they used to be. Our stories about America are also a tight fit. Since the Vietnam war our American dreams and national heroic mission as saviors of democracy have fallen into serious self-doubt and disrepute. How in the world can so many in the world see us as bad guy imperialists? At home political factions have stories so far apart they can't agree or compromise. Even scientists are not always believed, especially their serialized revelations about Evolution and climate change. Skeptic believers dismiss them as fictions loaded with lies. For many the "news" is no longer journalism; "fake news" has very different stories to tell. All this untidiness makes it hard for a personal narrative to stabilize itself, or us. And the stories go on and on, so they don't end happily ever after the way they once did.

So how do I find stability and standing as I wobble uneasily on the grounds of shifting relativities? How do I process the inflow-glut resulting from the massive availability of information available with a finger click, and how do I square the internet's potential to make me virtually omniscient while making obvious how omnipotent I decidedly am not?

All this is going on in me while I'm sitting in the Mayo Clinic Emergency Room wondering what think about what my heart is making of me.

I'm no hero-saint and certainly have missed many of the marks I've set for myself, but there's a somewhat inconsistent consistency about the story I tell myself about myself. I've tried to invent myself as a kind and courteous character, and all that. I've tried to be an active and engaged citizen, thinking globally and acting locally, and all that. And if there's been a bottom line to my personal narrative, a dominant habit, it's that I want to *know*. More and better. I read and study, and I write because it helps me align the swirls in my brain to neat sentences on a page. That way I can better see what I think. Do I write fictions? Yes. Do I make things up? Do I invent characters? Yes. But what I write represents, for me, some revelation of the knowledge-hungry true story I try to tell as I'm living in it. A long teaching career has enabled me to perform and professionalize my way of seeing myself.

But as I lay in the ER bed trying to hear my heartbeat my true story about myself suddenly took an weird turn. I know I'm going to die someday as we (others) certainly must, but still my life wasn't supposed to end like this, or soon, or (frankly) ever. And because it might end very soon it wouldn't have what every good story requires, a satisfying closure for its hero, me. Nurses and aides are coming and going, the colors of the chairs and walls are dull, and the trees outside the window keep swaying in the breeze. Everything continues being ordinary, and the death experience I now face is suddenly unthinkable and underwhelmed by the ordinary. Strangely too, there is no alarm or fear. The fact that I certainly will die, perhaps that same day, triggers no terror in me. But there is a concern: If my life history has been so clueless about what I am now facing, is there something bottomlessly defective with it? If so, have I wasted my life?

I think about my story's bottom line—the need to know—that is, pursue knowing to the end. And it is easy to conclude it has been a silly and shortsighted quest. I know the Promethean and Faustian myths well enough, how the knowledge hunger these figures tried to satisfy created misery not only for themselves but others. Prometheus—his name means "Foresight," as if knowledge provides it—stole fire from Zeus in order to better woeful humanity. His theft got him chained to a rock, forever. The various Fausts sold their souls to gain forbidden knowledge, the earlier ones selfishly pursuing it for its own sake, and Goethe's enlightened Faustus also was devoted to the improvement of humanity. In time these knowledge-thief types metamorphose into Dr. Frankenstein, scientist with good intentions with a curiosity so out of control he creates a pathetic monster who visits horrifying unintended consequences on the community. To go from Dr. Frankenstein to the genius physicists who have given us the H-bomb, genetic engineering, cloning and digital technologies requires no long leap of the imagination. Present trends seem potentially catastrophic in unprecedented ways, with new technologies being unleashed at the speed, not so metaphorically, of light.

What I carried into the Mayo Clinic ER with my ailing heart was not my personal disaster but the planet's, a runaway curiosity and obsession with technological innovation with major links to profit-making. I wondered, there in the presence of the latest devices that could save my life, if knowledge adventures were likely to destroy the world.

The politics of the question is especially troubling. As a university professor I've seen many teachers, writers and researchers who live in stories much like mine. Their mission is to learn, know, educate, communicate. Many have lived their whole lives devoted to that mission. Know-nothing politics—and its Fake News narrative—is now busy invalidating everything I, and my conscientious colleagues, deeply believe.

To stare at this prospect with a very troubled heart is to stand uneasily on the rim of a bottomless black hole in which no tendril of knowledge is visible. Death is the deepest and most final ignorance, and in the end we all end up falling into it. It's deeply troubling to imagine my personal quest, my citizenship, and my professional life descending into that black hole and disappearing into its meaninglessness. Call it existential despair.

Call this prospect also the heartbeat of the beast of the new Know-Nothing Fake News narrative found so deeply entertaining by millions of Americans. Bad politics was my ER catalyst for a descent into end-of-life despair.

The Know-Nothing in me whispers that I can solve my despair problem easily enough by subscribing to other-worldly belief—heaven and hell. All I need is belief in heaven and hell as after-life options. What can the knower in me honestly say in response? Only that knowledge and belief are as far apart as notions of heaven and hell. I can't believe what I can't know.

My rather sudden appearance in the ER places me in a limbo of sorts. The room is shiny and highly professionalized, and I feel banal in it, surrounded by no-nonsense business as usual technologies, furnishings, and uniformed personnel, all of them providing socially sincere smiles whenever possible. My extraordinary act of maybe dying is happening in an ordinary scene that the workers here redundantly take home with them on a daily basis. I feel like a body object been leered at, with no one desiring me and some no doubt quietly turned off. And the odd thing is that I'm rather bored with it all. I don't feel alarmed, or scared, or excited by what's happening to me. But I am curious: I want to *know* what's happening.

My desire to know is a consolation that grinds against my worry that the life-giving potential of technologies will be outweighed by their wholesale expropriation for exploitation and trouble making. At the core of my concern is that human curiosity is out of control, self-censored to be indifferent to unintended consequences, and too often driven by profit, power, or ego motives. If I 'm curious about how seeds can be engineered to increase yield and resist weeds, how can I not be curious about whether all weeds and pests can be eliminated from the planet? Why then would I worry about whether weeds and pests are *necessary* to the planet's well being? If I can split an atom, how can I not be curious about whether a stockpile of H-bombs can deter a nuclear attack? But how can I not also deeply concern myself with the possibility that a terrorist will make a nuclear device small enough to pack in a briefcase and powerful enough to destroy New York City? If I'm curious about my health and genetics, how can I not conduct genomic research that may help scientists create a new super-race of human beings, perhaps (unlike me, born too soon) someday immortal? Why should I worry about who will qualify for the new techno-immortality, and who (or what algorithm) will push the appropriate buttons? If I'm so hungry to know, how can I not be elated by the explosion of digital technologies that make information retrieval almost instantaneous? Why worry that a world-wide web of interlaced technologies may fail or be subverted, in ways that may block out massive life support systems and lead to totalitarian rule?

Is curiosity licentious when it lacks a conscience and sense of history?

My heart problem came swiftly on, it seems, and silently, secretly, as if it had no history or origin. Its visitation, I suspect, is natural, and I know for certain what nature eventually will do to me. I hear how natural I am when I listen to my heartbeat via a technological device—my heart's pulses sloshing back and forth like soggy clothes in my mother's old washing machine. My heart's untidiness takes me outdoors, beyond the buildings and traffic to forests, fields, and rivers, the ebbing and flowing, the buzz of insects, the silent digging of worms, the beautiful, and unpredictable, designs made by schools of fish in coral reefs, the sloshing of seas, and the strangely beautiful small monsters that live beneath reefs. And when I know enough to think about it, I pay attention to the invisible winds that toss and turn the trees outside the walls and windows of the building I'm in, the tree motions so fluid compared to the static symmetry of the building I'm in. I envision millions of peasants moving from dirty small plots of land into gigantic high-rise flats. I see cities enduring out of control mushroom growth. I see these cities fogged in veils of car exhaust. I see the brilliant colors blue and green fading into grey. I see Progress everywhere, with Nature on a sickbed, shriveled.

And I—my studies and teaching, my colleagues, my university, our knowledge quest—have enabled this dark conclusion. Could we have done otherwise? In a tragic narrative the suffering hero learns too late. Can we do some things better before it's too late? I ask myself if I've been foolish and too late.

I think of Henry Reed, a World War II veteran, who published a collection of poems entitled *Lessons of the War*. My favorite is "Naming of Parts," a darkly beautiful interior monologue describing a soldier's gun-cleaning protocol, a ritual duty required as flowers bloom and bees make their strange form of love to them. Reed weighs nature's ways against the iron requirements of the gun he is sworn to use: "The point of balance—we have not got." And yet I tell myself that a point of balance, though still unknown, may be known. I see information multiplying at a chain reaction rate as the world's population swells geometrically. I see my privacy going defunct, my individual movements tracked by invisible technologies. I see wars destroying great cities and small towns, and waves of refugees, with children and sacks on their backs, looking for somewhere to pause. I see how unfair life is, how fortunate I am to be in a bed in the Mayo Clinic ER, with life-giving people and technologies all around. I see human enterprise, indifferent to ignorance and Fake News claims, swelling out of control, while nature maintains its elemental motions and forms. Information, and what some call "knowledge," its parent, may be increasing at a space age rate, but the earth does not increase its area or change its direction around the sun. New chemistries may give us new remedies and thrills, but iron, magnesium and sodium are elements that remain elemental. These elements are in me too, and will remain with my remains, even as the earth continues to circulate.

I see myself among these remains, nosing the trend, as I've aged, toward self-disgust with my bodily functions. I, knowledge-seeker, must abide by the limits of my subject matter. There are limits--to knowledge too. Perhaps I've gone far enough in life, my presence and looming absence a necessary part of its balancing act. Perhaps the world has had too much of me, and the non-elemental may become useful as compost.

The point of balance we have not got: Where is it to be found? In the middle somewhere as we muddle along. It is one thing to desire knowledge in order to solve real and immediate human problems. But knowledge seeking is likely to go wrong when it stems from a need to dominate, usurp, control and own nature's sluggish life-giving ways. For the mad geniuses driven by profit motives and prestige inadequacy, the point of balance is more likely to be found in paths where knowledge is dedicated to maintaining natural healing ways rather than replacing them. The point of balance will be difficult to negotiate, given the current popularity of speed and acceleration and the bold ambitions of researchers and venture capitalists. Work slowdowns may be proper and necessary. Nature's ways are mysterious and slow, and the slow evolution of the high status humans currently enjoy as king of beasts suggests there are long-term benefits to going slow.

A slowdown might also help us locate a social point of balance. Let's call it modest living that prioritizes the elemental: Food, clothing, shelter, clean water, soil and air. Add family, friends and a sense of community and we have the basic elements of a satisfying life.

My strangest ER feeling is a sense of calm. I'm bemused by what's happening to me, and interested in what the dials are telling the health workers hovering over me. The workers seem reasonably contented, with moderate incomes. They seem conscientious, caring and knowing, mainly satisfied doing their work. I'm part of their ordinary hospital day, and they're trying to make things better for me.

I'd rather not explain my calm away as a symptom of debility, or of depression caused by failing capacities. Maybe the calm is grounded in a cockiness about how medical technology assures me I have nothing to worry about. I don't think so. I entered the ER with a conviction that the world is wacky and out of control, in part because of technology, and I find my calm oddly stabilizing in a world I see lacking a point of balance. I want to tell someone I think it's getting too late, but then I tell myself to remain silent and vigilant because there's a lot I don't know. So I'll let my calm speak for me.

Everybody Has One

+ v5n1

Tom Driscoll

Bought a crystal ball years ago in Antananarivo. I keep the orb on my desk cradled in a small rosewood pedestal. The size of an orange, it's slightly flawed, as if an encoded silicon wafer had been implanted, so I negotiated down the price asked by a tall, dark-eyed Malagasy woman wrapped head-to-toe in cobalt dyed cotton. *« N'essayez jamais de connaître la mort dans le cristal, »* she admonished while wrapping the prize in newsprint.

I asked her if she was trying to scare me. *« Tu ne peux pas voir la mort, peut tu, dans une boule? »*

« Peut-être, » she replied. *« Qu'est ça vous cherchez, monsieur? Cherchez-vous naissance et la mort? Mieux vous cherchez la connaissance et la vérité. »*

Well, here's the search result of *la connaissance et la vérité*: **Lost Lake Folk Opera** magazine, a Shipwreckt Books Publishing Company LLC imprint, has been publishing continuously for five years, providing a platform for some 250 writers, editors and photographers. This issue is significant for its sheer size, 120 pages, and quality content from 30 contributors, 6 of them past and present poets laureate, including the current Minnesota Laureate, Joyce Sutphen.

Pushing out two issues each year has been pretty demanding for this small literary press. Although I must say, producing *Folk Opera* is just about a perfect mash of fun and satisfaction, especially watching the quality of both magazine production and the content of submissions increase.

It's a perfect time to participate in American media. We are all cultural rapporteurs. Now is the time to raise and reassert the profile of writers in a literary scene crowded with performers and pundits. Now is not the time for any media outlet to yield.

∞

With every episode of the Donald Trump Reality Tragedy streaming nonstop into our consciousness from traditional and social media, I question whether there is anything anymore at all to sling into the street-fight of opinions about the President of the United States. Yet the thought of remaining silent is alien to me.

Keep in mind that my crystal ball is tuned into culture, and in it I see the dark flaw of a culture war smoldering up a miasmic fume. Culture is a spongy membrane, not a reinforced concrete wall that may crack and leak a little but otherwise constrains that which shall not be constrained: *la connaissance*.

To know in the crystal ball limitations on knowledge is to know the ultimate constraint of death, but to truly know *la mort* is to know *renaissance* as well. By my reckoning, art, and by definition, culture, cannot be murdered. Socio-political repression puts up walls, hand-shaped bricks of fear, hatred and economic subjugation, but always the walls crack and leak and eventually crumble from the pressure of that which shall not be constrained: *la vérité*.

To a festering old patrician like Donald Trump, the Grand Pooh-Bah of Culture War, the rise and inevitable fall of walls and civilizations is anathema; strikes fear into his heart – if it were a myocardial infarction or a spear. The Fall of Trump's Rome is already underway. In his crystal, *la connaissance* and *la vérité* are occluded by the toxic fires of populism, authoritarianism and fear.

Let's orient ourselves to where we're at in the early summer 2018 docudrama. Though the Muller investigation continues, everybody's talking about the separation of children from parents at the southern border, even after Trump stopped the practice with an executive order. Homeland Security secretary Kirstjen Nielsen was heckled at a Mexican restaurant in the Capitol and Melania Trump visited a youth detention center wearing a coat with a graffiti message on the back that read, "I really don't care. Do U?" Press secretary Sarah Sanders was refused service in a Virginia restaurant. Then the Supreme Court upheld Trump's travel ban, a Muslim ban by any other name. SCOTUS declined to rule on racial gerrymandering in Texas; ruled in favor of a Colorado baker who refused to decorate a cake for the marriage of a same sex couple; dealt a wakeup call to organized labor by overturning a 1977 Court decision that allowed unions to collect fees from non-union workers to fund activities like collective bargaining; and Justice Anthony Kennedy announced his retirement, giving Trump another opportunity to create a remorselessly conservative court, one that could control the judicial branch for decades.

The longer Trump and his willing enablers work to wreck our flawed but purposeful Federal Democracy with crowbars wielded by corporate conservatives, evangelical Christians and supremely angry agents of the white working class, the clearer becomes Mr. Trump's fundamental complaint—what's really bothering the depraved billionaire and his obsequious minions—**racial displacement, loss of privilege, and shrinking opportunity that threatens to redistribute American wealth.**

Arts funding will eventually become a well-defined Trump target. Artistic freedom is already under threat. The President has manipulated the NFL, turning the *National Anthem* into an obligatory patriotic display bordering on jingoism; all because Colin Kaepernick took a knee to express his personal concern over police shooting black men.

Trump is no crystal mirage. He's a demagogue. Artistic display of public discontent pisses him off. The Golden Globes, the Oscars and Tonys, as well as late night television; the Nation's presses, large and small—we've seen his angry tweets. Trump wants to control language and speech, constrain expression, build a wall around the diverse, rich and unbridled American culture. Don't let that happen. Non-violent, virulently imaginative artists can stop Mr. Trump. Use a secret handshake, give a furtive wink, and whisper: *À bas le despote.*

The Levee
Ken McCullough

The Levee: Then and Now
for Mayor Mark Peterson

"Eventually, all things merge into one, and a river runs through it.
The river was cut by the world's great flood and runs over rocks
from the basement of time."
—Norman McLean, from *A River Runs Through It*

If you took a time lapse photo of the levee
you'd see the cycles, the ebb and flow—
the river swollen from bluff to bluff
or shallow enough to herd your cattle to Wisconsin;
you'd see natives in dugouts, Frenchmen in pirogues,
and Capt. Orrin Smith, on the Nominee, looking for a landing.
Later, the faces of swells and high rollers, of presidents,
of scoundrels and confidence men
lolling on the decks of the riverboats.
You'd see thousands of steamboats and sternwheelers;
in recent times, the updates: the American Queen,
the Mississippi Queen, the Delta Queen,
the hullabaloo when the big boats are moored
to the heavy iron rings, the gangplanks set in place.
You'd talk to river captains, sitting on shaded benches
like Frank Fugina, Walter or Dick Karnath, hear their salty tales
even though they called themselves brown water sailors.
And if you listen closely, you can still hear the notes
of the calliope haunting its way upriver.

At the start, nothing but a sandbar, and several burial mounds,
and then the sprawling village of Wapasha's band.
You'd see visitors like popinjay Zebulon Pike,
who described the vista from Sugarloaf
or at least claimed to have gone up there.
You'd chat with Seth Eastman, soldier and artist, who sketched
a mock charge on his military detail by Wapasha's warriors—
afterwards, they had a good laugh then sat down to parlay;

You'd hear chatter from the summer lodges,
but those voices faded west when the land was ceded.
Claim shanties went up on Keoxa—hard words, fisticuffs,
eyes gouged, shots fired. The town dubbed Montezuma,
'til Henry Huff changed the name to Winona—

the town grew fast and slapdash. The sky grew black
and passenger pigeons crashed the branches with their weight.

In 1861 we stood on the levee to see our boys off
when they shipped out to fight the Rebs.
We can still hear the cheers, the snare drums and the oompah.
In more recent times, when the river crested at over 20 feet,
we looked out across the hissing cataract
and it made our hackles rise.
So we built up the wall, good to 22 feet.
Later, we watched Leo Smith and Peter Shortridge
assemble their Escheresque frieze along that levee wall—
like something fit for the Nile: it has served us well.

We were here on the levee when the Grand Excursion
made its way upriver in 1854, and again for the Sesquicentennial.
Ladies in their finery waved their hankies at us
and smiled coquettishly, and I blushed.
Piccolos and flutes chortled in the June breezes.

Many of us learned to swim across the way
at Latsch Island pavilion, lessons from Cabby McGill,
under watchful eyes of Lloyd Luke and that tanned
and trim lifeguard who became our mayor, Jerry Miller.
John Latsch, our benefactor, built the pavilion
so that young swimmers were safe in the roiling waters.

We've had our times on Latsch Island, on Wolf Spider Island.
And all of us wished we lived in boathouses there.
And countless years we've watched the fireworks
reflected in the river, the booms and explosions
the oohas and aahs, our kids on our shoulders.

Various bridges have come and gone—
we watched in horror as that first locomotive plunged into the river
and the bridge collapsed. No one died, no one injured.
Rebuilt in 1852 and stayed in use for 100 years—its skeleton survives.
Some boats had brief lives here like the James P. Pearson, (the Wilkie I),

the Wilkie II and the dredge William A. Thompson, an also-ran.
Listen for all the hot air expelled over the fates of these vessels.
Now, the streamlined Cal Fremling and Aaron Repinski's Winona Tour Boat
wait at anchor in their places.

This used to be the gateway to the west
when all the rafts of timber from upriver
wound up here, and sawdust filled the air.
Until they clear-cut the old growth white pine.
You can still smell sawdust when the wind is right.
All the wheat from west of here used to pass through
until the railroads cut into that market.
And now the long strings of monster barges
being pushed by tows, the deck hands, the steersman.
The ebb and flow, the ebb and flow.
The river is our highway once again.

In 1897 we built the gem of Riverside Park,
envied by all the river towns in America;
its geometrical promenades, its plantings—
But that faded into a ghost of itself.
We have watched lovers walking arm in arm
along the shady walkways, now and then a wedding,
echoes of banjos and fiddles, trumpets and accordions.
Yes, this used to be known as the gateway to the west—
Now, when we look out through this arch
we see that it is the gateway to the future—
the slumbering downtown come to life again.
And when we look through this arch
with its brilliant stained glass panels,
when we look toward the river, we see the history we share.
We'll see new art, hear new music, dance new dances,
in concert with the old, the river flowing in our veins.
Winona, the firstborn daughter, who adopted all of us,
is back to stay: "…all things merge into one,
and a river runs through it."

*Presented by the Poet Laureate of Winona on the occasion of the
Grand Opening of the revitalized Levee Park, June 24, 2018.*

www.ingramcontent.com/pod-product-compliance
Lightning Source LLC
Chambersburg PA
CBHW081147170626
46809CB00010B/3120